HAROLD BRODKEY
THE RUNAWAY SOUL

This man has been called America's greatest writer. On the evidence of two collections of short stories, he has been compared to Proust, Wordsworth and Milton. For more than 25 years, he has been working on a novel that has become, quite literally, his life's work.

THE RUNAWAY SOUL is finally here, lyrical, searing, lucid, epic, the most eagerly awaited first novel of all time.

Read it and decide for yourself whether Harold Brodkey is truly a great writer.

"One of the great brave journeys of American literature."

Don DeLillo

"Quite unlike anything in contemporary fiction. It is nakedly original."

James Wood, *The Guardian*

"Forget the Proust comparison, Brodkey is himself and many pages here have the deep rolling profound thrust, painterly originality, and lightning-bolt flash of great art."

Kirkus Reviews

Jonathan Cape   £15.99   ISBN 0224 03001 9

f l a m i n g o

Getting Used to Dying

Zhang Xianliang

Winner of the monthly *Independent* Foreign Fiction Award

'The Chinese Kundera'
NEW YORK REVIEW OF BOOKS

£4.99

The Arrow of Time

Peter Coveney & Roger Highfield

Top ten bestseller now in Flamingo

'More comprehensive and more accessible than *A Brief History of Time* and much better value'
T.L.S.

£5.99

Midnight Mass

Paul Bowles

From the bestselling author of *The Sheltering Sky*

'His short stories are among the best ever written by an American'
GORE VIDAL £4.99

Sudden Fiction International

Sixty Short Stories

Edited by Robert Shapard and James Thomas

'My thanks for giving us so many wonderful voices in an accessible and delightful presentation. They're perfect bed-time reading.'
AMY TAN £5.99

The Female Eunuch

Germaine Greer

The bible of the women's movement, updated with a new foreword.

'The best feminist book so far'
NEW YORK TIMES £5.99

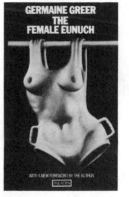

GRANTA

WE'RE SO HAPPY!

38

Editor: Bill Buford
Deputy Editor: Tim Adams
Managing Editor: Ursula Doyle
Editorial Assistant: Robert McSweeney

Managing Director: Derek Johns
Financial Controller: Geoffrey Gordon
Promotions and Advertising: Sally Lewis

Picture Editor: Alice Rose George
Design: Chris Hyde
Executive Editor: Pete de Bolla
Contributing Editor: Lucretia Stewart
US Associate Publisher: Anne Kinard, Granta, 250 West 57th Street, Suite 1316, New York, NY 10107.

Editorial and Subscription Correspondence: Granta, 2–3 Hanover Yard, Noel Road, Islington, London N1 8BE. Telephone: (071) 704 9776. Fax: (071) 704 0474. Subscriptions: (071) 837 7765.
A one-year subscription (four issues) is £19.95 in Britain, £25.95 for the rest of Europe, and £31.95 for the rest of the world.
All manuscripts are welcome but must be accompanied by a stamped, self-addressed envelope or they cannot be returned.

Granta is printed in the United States of America. The paper used in this publication meets the minimum requirements of American National Standard for Information Sciences—Permanence of Paper for Printed Library Materials, ANSI Z39.48-1984 ∞

Granta is published by Granta Publications Ltd and distributed by Penguin Books Ltd, Harmondsworth, Middlesex, England; Viking Penguin, a division of Penguin Books USA Inc, 375 Hudson Street, New York, NY 10014, USA; Penguin Books Australia Ltd, Ringwood, Victoria, Australia; Penguin Books Canada Ltd, 2801 John Street, Markham, Ontario, Canada L3R 1BR; Penguin Books (NZ) Ltd, 182-190 Wairau Road, Auckland 10, New Zealand. This selection copyright © 1991 by Granta Publications Ltd.

Cover by Senate. Photo: Eve Arnold (Magnum)

Granta 38, Winter 1991
ISBN 0-14-015210-5

BLOODY MARGARET

THREE POLITICAL FANTASIES BY
MARK LAWSON

Hardback
UK Publication date
8 November 1991

She's back... but don't worry, it's only fiction. On the first anniversary of the Iron Lady's downfall, Mark Lawson marks his fictional debut with three political fantasies:

The Nice Man Cometh – inspired by a new political party, the Nice People attempt a peaceful takeover of Britain...

Bloody Margaret – the entourage of a British Prime Minister, including her rivals, her bodyguards, her porcelain cleaner and her electric shock consultant – recall their part in her rise and fall...

And *Teach Yourself American In Seven Days* – besieged by Americans, a London banker becomes involved in a horrifying rewrite of Kafka's *Metamorphosis*.

SONGS OF THE DOOMED

Dr. Hunter S. Thompson

More 'Notes on the Death of the American Dream', as Dr. Hunter S. Thompson recalls high and hideous moments in his own life (and the lives of many others) in the third extraordinary volume of the Gonzo Papers.

Hardback
UK Publication Date
11 October 1991

CARVER COUNTRY

Tess Gallagher

A beautiful record of one of America's finest writers, with text selected from Carver's short stories, poems and unpublished letters and photographs by Bob Adelman, who corresponded with Carver about the project until the writer's death in 1988.

Hardback
UK Publication Date
22 November 1991

THE JAMES CRUMLEY COLLECTION

James Crumley

Containing James Crumley's three most famous detective novels, all of which have long been out of print; *The Wrong Case, The Last Good Kiss* and *Dancing Bear*.

'Crumley has become the foremost living writer of private-eye fiction'

CRIME AND MYSTERY WRITERS

Hardback
UK Publication Date
8 November 1991

PICADOR

OUTSTANDING INTERNATIONAL WRITING

CONTENTS

Odyssey

Rediscover the adventure of travel to faraway destinations with a major new series of travel books. ODYSSEY GUIDES (Hong Kong) has already published over 30 titles, from MOSCOW and LENINGRAD in the Soviet Union to SAN FRANCISCO and LAS VEGAS in the United States. Our coverage of Southeast Asia is without compare.

Guides

Every book contains a solid introduction, practical information, the finest colour photography available, and generous excerpts from both classic and unconventional literary sources such as Teddy Roosevelt (in the Philippines), Charlie Chaplin (in Bali) or Bruce Chatwin (in Hong Kong). What better way to prepare for embarking on an *Odyssey?*

Trade sales and distribution by Hodder & Stoughton Publishers, Mill Road, Dunton Green, Sevenoaks, Kent TN13 2YA

BILL MORRIS
MOTORAMA 1954

It was at sundown on New Year's Day 1954 that Claire Hathaway began to feel embarrassed by her new television set.

The Rose Parade was on the screen, but she couldn't take her eyes off the set itself. It was a twenty-one-inch RCA console with a gumwood cabinet and nubby brown fabric over the speakers, and it dwarfed the other furniture in her living-room. She had gone downtown yesterday to buy a party dress and had come home with this thing instead.

Her guests seemed to be in awe of it. No one spoke as the camera zoomed in on the last car in the parade, a glittering Cadillac convertible with gobs of chrome and little fluttering American flags and President Dwight Eisenhower and his wife Mamie in the back seat. The President and First Lady were smiling and waving to the crowd. The Cadillac was beige. The Eisenhowers' clothes were beige. Their faces were beige.

Norm Slenski started for the kitchen with his empty beer glass. He belched into his fist and said, 'Hey, what gives? I thought this was supposed to be one of them new *color* TVs.'

Everyone laughed except his wife. Wanda was the only person in the room who didn't design Buicks for a living and drink heavily on holidays. She hadn't moved from her spot at the end of the sofa or uncrossed her legs for over an hour. 'Norm,' she said, 'that next beer's your limit.'

'Right-e-o,' he called over his shoulder.

From her seat on the sofa, Claire could see him in the kitchen. He put ice cubes in a tall glass, filled it nearly to the brim with Scotch, then darkened it with a splash of Coca-Cola. He returned to the sofa and patted his wife on the knee. 'Might as well go ahead and switch to Cokes now,' he said.

Claire wished Norm and Wanda and everyone else would go home. But that was out of the question, she knew, because she'd invited them to watch the Rose Bowl two weeks earlier, the day they learned that the commercial for the new Buick Century would air during half-time. Now her apartment was full of half-drunk car stylists mesmerized by a washed-out sepia image of Ike and Mamie, and all Claire could think about was last night.

There was something she needed to remember, but toward

midnight her mind had grown blurry. She had no idea how she got home; around noon, she awoke on the sofa with a dry mouth and a throbbing headache, still wearing her green dress and high heels and pearls.

The day after Christmas, Harvey Pearl, the head of General Motors styling, had strolled up to her drawing table and casually asked if she would like to accompany him to Ted Mackey's New Year's Eve party; Ted Mackey was the general manager of the Buick Division. It was the first time in her four years with the company that Harvey Pearl had said a word to her.

She had been the youngest person at the party, but the drinks helped her relax, and she was grateful when a neighbor of the Mackeys, who said he'd made 'a nice little bundle in ball-bearings,' cornered her by the fireplace and insisted on telling her about his recent trip abroad.

'Those Japs are doing some amazing things,' he said, unable to take his eyes off her bare shoulders. 'I keep telling Ted and Harvey that those Japs are up to something. But nobody at GM ever listens. They already know everything.'

Well before midnight, Claire noticed a Negro maid helping Mrs Mackey up the stairs. That was the last thing Claire remembered clearly. Now, watching the beige Eisenhowers wave at the crowd in Pasadena, she tried to retrieve scraps from the rest of the evening. On her way to the bathroom she bumped into Harvey Pearl, who was telling a group of blue-haired women that Claire was the top designer in the entire Buick studio. He was shouting and spilling his drink. Then there was an explosion—someone had thrown a glass into the fireplace. Everyone roared. Claire made her get-away and locked the bathroom door behind her. She spent a long time touching up her hair and make-up and admiring the brass fixtures, the black marble sink, the bright fluffy towels. The wallpaper was rough, like straw or grass. She had never been inside such a house before, with its thick carpets, dark panelling, twinkling whisky decanters, lake view and a roaring fire fed by four-foot logs. She liked the living-room best, especially the Persian rug and the Franz Kline painting, ancient geometries formed by bold black slashes on a blinding white sky. When Ted Mackey saw her admiring it, he walked up and said, 'So give me an artist's opinion. Is it worth a damn?'

'It's . . . it's gorgeous.' She felt herself blushing. 'Is it an original?'

He chuckled. 'I sure as hell hope so. We bought it at an auction in New York last summer—my wife did, that is. You could buy a couple of fully loaded Cadillacs with what I paid for it.' He cocked his head and studied the painting.

The thing she was trying to remember then came back to her. After the encounter with Harvey Pearl and the yawning old ladies, Claire had stepped out of the bathroom and walked straight into Ted Mackey's chest. He was wearing a herring-bone blazer, a white shirt and a red tie. He smelled of wood-smoke. Without a word he had taken her shoulders in his hands and kissed her firmly on the lips.

'It's midnight,' he said. 'Happy New Year.'

He released her shoulders and walked down the hall to the living-room, where everyone was standing in front of the TV set yelling. The ball was falling on to the throng in Times Square.

Claire now forced herself to concentrate on the parade. Ike and Mamie were waving and smiling; they looked beige.

Everyone cheered. So this was color TV. The snow may have been whistling horizontally off the Great Lakes, and Detroit may have been sinking into another freezing midwinter dusk, but thousands of miles away in Pasadena the sun was buttery and gold, and girls in bright red suits tossed batons, and the President and First Lady rode through the sunshine in a purring General Motors product, waving and smiling. It was a paid holiday. There was plenty of beer in the refrigerator, and snacks and dips were on the coffee-table. There was color TV. And Claire Hathaway had, at last, remembered the taste of Ted Mackey's kiss.

2

Six miles to the north, in a white house on the edge of Mirror Lake, Ted Mackey watched the Rose Bowl kick-off. The game

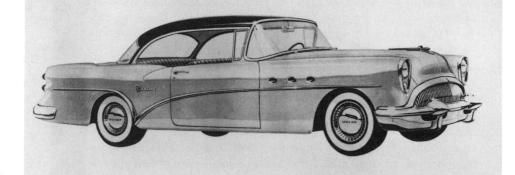

normally made him tingle, especially when Michigan was playing, but he watched it dully. Like everyone who has ever thrown a party, Ted had spent much of the day reliving the night before. The roster of business associates, neighbors, golf and gin rummy buddies and their wives had showed up and filled the house with smoke and chatter. Don Cloesy, the biggest Buick dealer in Detroit, had shouted at his wife and stormed out of the house, leaving her in tears to find a ride home with friends. Walter Koether, who'd sold the house to Ted and built an even bigger one across the lake, passed out briefly on the sofa but rallied for midnight. Someone had tossed a highball glass into the fireplace.

There was also Claire Hathaway.

Ted had seen her in the design studio at the Tech Center, but she always looked severe, almost tomboyish. She never wore make-up and dressed in loose sweaters, pleated skirts and scuffed loafers. When he greeted her in the foyer, he was astonished: the electric green dress, the red hair, the milky shoulders, the throat. She was wearing pearls. And she wobbled, suddenly several inches taller, on high heels. He found himself sharing Harvey's obvious delight at the way the arrival of such a hot property had inspired sudden ardor in the men and sudden suspicion in their wives.

The football settled into the Stanford player's arms at his own goal-line.

'Kill him!' Ted roared. 'Take his head off!'

The Michigan defenders, in blue jerseys and yellow pants, stormed downfield, and six of them stopped the Stanford ball carrier at the fifteen yard line, an ugly, audible crunch. The football squirted into the air, and a Michigan player snatched it and ran into the endzone.

'Touchdown! Michigan touchdown!' Ted yelled, jumping up and spilling Scotch on the Persian rug. 'Harvey, you sure you don't want to back out of that bet?'

Harvey Pearl didn't answer. He was looking over snapshots of the war that Milmary had dug out of the attic. Harvey hated football. He hated most things that Detroit car people worshipped: violent sports, cocktail parties, stag hunting trips in northern Michigan.

At half-time Ted hollered into the dining-room that their commercial was about to come on.

The screen showed a country road. There was a low roar and a distant unidentifiable dot. The dot became a car, their car, the one Harvey Pearl had nursed through the Byzantine design process, and the one that would be Ted Mackey's greatest triumph or his greatest disaster. Ted and Harvey had seen this car many times over the past three years: first in crude sketches, then more refined ones, then as a clay model, as a full-blown motorized prototype and finally as a mass-produced wonder clicking off the Flint assembly line. It was moving fast now, getting bigger and louder. A voice began: 'We at the Buick Division of General Motors are proud to bring back a piece of our illustrious past.'

The front of the car was a confection of dazzling chrome: headlight sockets like sad droopy eyes, a grille like a frowning mouth with its metal teeth exposed, and a front bumper that looked as if it could scoop dead cows off the road. The car was hot pink.

'After a twelve-year absence, the Buick Century is back. It's destined to be the car of the year, a sports car the whole family will enjoy, and it's at a Buick dealer near you.'

It shrank toward the sunset.

Ted whooped with joy. He put his drink down, gave Harvey Pearl a bear-hug and led him in an impromptu jig.

'You liked it?' Harvey Pearl said, smoothing his jacket and straightening his bow-tie.

'I *loved* it! Come on, you gotta admit, wasn't she sexy?'

'Oh yes, she was sexy, all right.'

'And didn't she look just a little bit dangerous?'

'Oh yes.'

Milmary picked up her Bloody Mary. 'While you fellows pat each other on the back, I'm going to get some champagne.'

Ted was beside himself. He'd been waiting for this moment for three years, and for once in his life an event had lived up to his gargantuan expectations. He switched channels to the Cotton Bowl, where it was also half-time. After a commercial for Altes beer, the screen filled with capital letters: PLYMOUTH. Ted turned

up the volume. It was their prime competition. Plymouth was number three in sales behind Chevy and Ford. The narrator spoke of 'elegant appointments' and 'Turbo-torque power', as the camera circled a dumpy blue four-door sedan on a suburban street.

'No energy,' Harvey Pearl said. 'No sex.'

Then the camera froze. Ted and Harvey saw it at the same instant: the Plymouth's front bumper was a virtual replica of the Buick's, down to the two pointed bulbs. Neither man said a word. They were thinking the same horrible thought: Plymouth had pirated Buick's design work.

Milmary swept into the room with a bottle of champagne and three long-stemmed glasses. She looked at the men, at the television screen, at the dumpy blue car.

'What's the matter?' she said. 'You seen a ghost?'

3

Morey Caan lived alone with a gelded yellow cat named Fat Boy on P Street in Georgetown in Washington, D.C.—'safely upwind from the seat of American power'—and while he generally enjoyed the feeling that he was the last bachelor in America, holidays were rough. Morey especially disliked New Year's Day because he always felt fine and the rest of the world was busy recuperating from what he called Amateur Night. It wasn't that he condemned people for wearing stupid hats and getting knee-walking drunk and vomiting in the wrong places. It was just that he had never developed a taste for alcohol—an achievement for someone who had grown up in the South, spent four years at the University of Virginia, a training ground for problem drinkers, and worked for the past eight years amid that massive army of boozers and misfits known as the Washington press corps.

Morey had been on the phone most of the day, and his ear felt like a cauliflower. After talking to his father, his sister, his brother-in-law, his niece, his nephew, after shouting a few pleasantries to his stone-deaf grandmother, it was time to call his best friend, Will Lomax, in Detroit.

Until four years ago, Will had been Morey's room-mate and one of the stars of the Washington press corps, the hardest worker and drinker, and the most tireless skirt-chaser. Nothing seemed beyond him. After graduating with Morey from Virginia, Will rose from a lowly bureau job with the *Atlanta Constitution* to a highly visible one with the *Washington Post* in less than two years; and in less than a year at the *Post*, he put together a series of articles on the local numbers rackets that nearly won him a Pulitzer Prize. Will found himself roaming the corridors of the Capitol, where doors began to open magically before him.

And then Morey landed a job covering cops for the *Post*, and the two were inseparable. They showed up together at the Press Club bar, at cocktail parties, press conferences, Senators' ball games. Will always led the way, fluid and lanky, his hair as black and shiny as patent leather; he had a soft drawl and lock-up-your-daughter looks. Morey tagged along behind, the nebbish kid-brother type with the rumpled clothes and exploding hair and greasy eyeglasses that looked as though they had been fished out of day-old dish-water.

Then, one raw January day in 1950, Will Lomax walked into the Press Club bar and announced he was getting married and changing jobs. To top it off, he was passing over the Social Register lovelies and marrying a social worker named Margaret Mason from 'West-by-God Virginia', as he put it, and taking a flack job with General Motors and moving to Detroit.

The going-away party at the Press Club was like a wake, and Morey got so drunk he vomited on the geraniums by the elevator.

But Will stayed in touch over the next four years. He visited when he was in Washington on business—more often than either of them expected thanks to the 1952 election—and they spoke regularly on the phone, usually on GM's nickel. Will had spent months trying to persuade Morey to write a free-lance magazine article about the completely redesigned line of 1954 Buicks, especially the new Century. He wanted the article to appear in *Life*.

Morey pinched the bridge of his nose and dialled the number in Detroit.

'Hello?' came a woman's voice from the fuzzy dells of West-by-God Virginia.

'Margaret, it's Morey calling from Washington. Happy New Year!'

'Well, happy New Year to you too, Morey. Hold on. Will's right here.'

The phone clattered on the table. As is so often the case with abandoned bachelors, Morey could not comprehend his best friend's choice of a wife. He could see her wearing a flowery apron; it would be snowing outside, and a roast with potatoes and carrots and onions would be in the oven. She had brittle brown hair and a high smooth forehead whose utter blankness led Morey to suspect, perhaps unfairly, that she had never had a troubling or intelligent thought in her life. Granted, the woman had a tremendous body. But why had Will Lomax gone and married it?

Will's voice boomed over the telephone line. 'What you up to, boy?'

'Not much, old man,' Morey said. 'Just wanted to wish everyone a happy New Year.' He could hear babies. 'What are you doing besides changing diapers?'

'Nursing a hangover and watching Michigan win another Rose Bowl, like everyone else in *Dee*-troit.'

'How's the book?'

Morey never failed to ask about *The Book*—the insider's story of the Buick Division he'd been urging Will Lomax to write for the past four years. As envisioned by Morey, it would chronicle the behind-the-scenes machinations of the largest industrial empire in the world, exposing sales hustles and management callousness and blowing the lid off the myth that GM was as tightly run as Bismarck's army. It would also make Will Lomax a bundle of money that would buy him his one-way ticket out of what he called 'the frozen hell-hole', the great city of Detroit.

'I ain't done diddly on *The Book*,' Will said.

'Why the hell not?'

Opposite: Roy Cohn, Joe McCarthy and G. David Schine

'I got another promotion.'

'And another raise?'

'Naturally. On Monday I'll be working directly for Ted Mackey. His very own PR drone.'

'The Great White Shark himself! Will, that'll be perfect for *The Book*!'

Morey expected more, but what came was the low grumble of static. Finally he said, 'What's wrong, old man?'

'To tell you the truth, I'm scared shitless.'

'Why? You've got twice as much brains as Ted Mackey, who's only a glorified salesman. Think about it. You'll be right there in the inner sanctum.'

'I know that. But you've got no idea what Mackey's like. He's a maniac. He eats people alive. He—aw, forget it. I'll be fine. How's *your* book coming along?'

The night after the 1952 election, Morey, too, had started writing a book. The working title was *Straight from the Horse's Mouth*. It was to be a series of direct quotations from Ike himself, verbatim gobbledegook, double-talk and gibberish, an encyclopaedia of Ike-speak. While Morey understood that buffoonery in high places was not new, he believed he had a responsibility to alert a dozing populace to its contemporary brand, Ike's brand, and expose the President of the United States for what he was: a five-star moron.

Morey eyed the untouched stack of periodicals and newspapers beside his typewriter. He had promised himself that today would be the day he read, clipped and sorted them. Now, in addition to feeling sad and lonely, he felt guilty.

'I've been pretty busy myself lately,' he said. 'Been to Baraboo, Wisconsin, working on a piece for the *Saturday Review* about the "Joe Must Go" movement, a bunch of guys who hate McCarthy's guts—' He heard a loud crash, followed by the bawling of two babies and Margaret's yelling.

'Listen,' Will said, 'I gotta jump. An H-bomb just landed in the kitchen sink. You keep in touch now, y'hear?'

'Will do.' Morey hung up—and sat, oblivious to the coffee cups and the sandwich rinds with their blooms of blue mould. He had one thing to be cheerful about: in the new issue of *Time*,

James Hagerty, Ike's press secretary, said that he would allow reporters to quote the President directly at press conferences. This was a breakthrough. It was the subject of a Sunday *New York Times* editorial: 'The widest dissemination of the news is all to the good. But there is the danger that the participants will become mere actors in a gigantic show, and that goes both for the newspaper-men who ask the questions and the presidents who answer them.'

Morey enjoyed the ironies. There's a new bomb that can blow a hole in the ocean floor, and the Russians are sure to have one as well, but the President's two worries are balancing the federal budget and his golf swing. Who cares? Inflation's low, employment's high, everyone loves the Republican in the White House, and they're so busy buying cars and making money and babies that they might as well be embalmed—even guys like Will Lomax, the original cowboy. And the best the *New York Times* can do is fret that reporters and presidents are in danger of becoming actors in a big-top freak show.

4

The carpet in Ted Mackey's office was the color of brushed steel and so plush it swallowed Will Lomax's footsteps and gave him the sensation that he was walking on air. As he crossed the room, he saw that the lace on his brightly polished right shoe was about to come untied.

Ted was smoking a Chesterfield. It was not yet eight o'clock, but already there were three butts in the glass ashtray. The only other things on Ted's desk were a black telephone and the latest issue of *Photoplay*. Ted was reading Hedda Hopper's prediction that Joe DiMaggio and Marilyn Monroe would marry by the end of January.

'Morning,' Ted said without looking up. 'Have a seat. Harvey Pearl and John Nickles are on their way.'

Will sat in a green leather chair in the corner and crossed his legs, trying to hide his unravelled right shoe-lace. Snow whipped past the big windows, blotting out the city, as if someone had pulled a gauze curtain over the first workday of the year.

Ted Mackey's lips moved as he read. Will knew that his new boss fantasized about Marilyn Monroe and dreamed of hiring her either as 'the Buick Girl' for an ad campaign later in the year, when the sales war with Plymouth would get bare-knuckled vicious, or as 'the Wildcat Girl', emblem of the two-seat sports car he was so eager to develop. Hiring Marilyn Monroe was, depending on who you believed, the greatest idea since ball-bearings or else a guaranteed one-way ticket to the funny farm. Will Lomax wasn't sure what he thought about it, but knew from numerous late-night discussions over numerous drinks that it was an obsession with Ted Mackey.

'She's perfect,' Ted said, yanking his necktie loose and pounding the table. 'She's everything we want these new Buicks to be—gorgeous, sexy, dangerous, but not *too* dangerous. That's what makes a new car sell. You don't believe me, ask any dealer. Those guys understand. But don't try to tell those fucking accountants on the Finance Committee. They'll tell you Marilyn Monroe's just another one of my hunches and they need to study it. Jesus! We've got a chance to sign the hottest piece of ass in Hollywood for the hottest car of the year—and those assholes want to *study* it!'

Then there was the calendar. Pinned to the door inside Ted's private office bathroom was Marilyn Monroe's famous nude calendar shot, the one of her stretched out on her right side, swaddled in red velvet, looking over her shoulder with her mouth slightly open. Whenever a first-time visitor—a union boss, an executive, a reporter, a politician, one of Ted's sports cronies —emerged from that bathroom, Ted would regale him with the astonishing economics of the calendar: six million copies were printed; the distributor made 750,000 dollars; the photographer made 900 dollars; and Marilyn made fifty dollars. If the woman's value exceeded her cost, Will understood, that made her all the more attractive to the general manager of the Buick Division.

Ted slipped the *Photoplay* into his bottom desk drawer as Harvey Pearl and John Nickles strode into the office. The two men could not be more different. Harvey Pearl was a dandy, a eek ending January 16 1954   EVERY THURSDAY 3½ᴰ

Picturegoer

HE NATIONAL FILM WEEKLY

They're Giving Monroe A New Look

see page 8

cocky little tyrant who'd had a hand in designing more than thirty million GM cars over a quarter century, the visionary who had given Detroit its greatest money-maker since mass production: the annual model change. He wore his hair in a brush cut and favored bow-ties and suspenders and flamboyant suits that strayed a long way from the corporate uniform of dark blue.

John Nickles was textbook General Motors. He was the head of Buick styling; his claim to fame was the 'ventiports', the notched chrome holes in the front quarter panels that served no purpose but had become a Buick trade mark. Three ventiports made the car a 'three-holer', a Special or a Century, while the Roadmaster was a 'four-holer': big body, big engine, the true status boat. John Nickles had a lumpy bald head and wore drab suits, white shirts and black shoes. Will had never seen him laugh.

When they were seated, Ted stood up, clamped his hands behind his back and paced in front of the windows. Will expected something about Joe DiMaggio and Marilyn Monroe. But instead Ted said, 'I trust everyone saw our commercial during the Rose Bowl.'

Will Lomax twisted in his chair. The tone of Ted's voice reminded him why he'd dreaded this moment. He felt clammy and tired.

'And I trust everyone saw the Plymouth commercial during the Cotton Bowl,' Ted said.

Harvey and John nodded.

'Well, for your information, the fucking Plymouth's front bumper is a spittin' image of ours. That means one thing: we've got a design leak. And that means for the next four years we're going to sit around with our thumbs up our asses wondering how much Plymouth knows about our designs. We spend forty-two million dollars on this project'—he looked straight at Will—'and now we're *fucked*!'

5

The first thing Marilyn Monroe did on her wedding-day was peroxide her pubic hair with a tooth-brush. Though she had once told reporters she liked feeling blonde 'all over', she did not mention that 'all over' included the troublesome wedge of dark curls between her legs. On her wedding day, she dunked a tooth-brush into a bottle of hydrogen peroxide, then dabbed and stroked the thatch until it was a uniform, fluffy blonde. Marilyn Monroe was determined to be blonde all over when she was carried across the threshold by her second husband, the famed Yankee Clipper, Joe DiMaggio.

The second thing Marilyn did on her wedding-day was phone Harry Brand in Los Angeles. She told Brand, the publicity boss at Twentieth Century Fox, that after a two-year run in the gossip sheets she was finally going to make all the rumors come true. She would be marrying Joe DiMaggio that afternoon at one o'clock in San Francisco City Hall. She asked Brand to tell all her friends. He promptly called every gossip columnist he could think of, then the Associated Press, United Press, International News Syndicate and the major television and radio networks.

The bride and groom showed up at City Hall in San Francisco a few minutes before one. He wore an impeccably tailored dark blue suit. She wore a simple brown suit and a black satin coat with an ermine collar. He was accompanied by Reno Barsochinni, his best man and manager of his restaurant at Fisherman's Wharf, and Frank 'Lefty' O'Doul, an old baseball crony. Marilyn arrived alone. Well, not exactly alone. There was also a mob of reporters, photographers and fans waiting in the third-floor corridor, and they peppered the couple with questions about their honeymoon and the number of children they intended to have, and with repeated requests that they kiss for the cameras. When the ceremony was delayed to allow a clerk to type the marriage license, Marilyn slipped into a phone booth.

She called her favorite gossip columnist, Sidney Skosky, but got no answer. Finally she got through to Kendis Rochlen, a Los Angeles free-lancer. They chatted for a while, then Rochlen asked the one question that mattered to her: 'So tell me, Marilyn, how do you *feel*?'

'Oh, Kendis,' she whispered, 'I'm so happy. I have sucked my last cock!'

When Marilyn returned, DiMaggio, not yet married and already exasperated, snapped: 'OK, let's get this marriage going.'

Judge Charles Peery appealed for quiet, and a hush fell over the newsmen and the crowd. The ceremony lasted three minutes. When it was over, the photographers asked the newly-weds to kiss. They did. The photographers asked them to kiss again. They did. And again, until finally DiMaggio grabbed his wife by the arm and, with Reno and Lefty running interference, pushed his way to a waiting blue Cadillac and the couple sped off south.

Joe DiMaggio, the son of a fisherman, was now the husband of . . . Marilyn Monroe, offspring of orphanages and foster homes: she had married for the first time at sixteen, then took up jobs modelling and acting, playing a cannery worker, a disturbed baby-sitter, a sexy secretary, a hooker, a borderline hysteric and finally an air-headed blonde in *Gentlemen Prefer Blondes* and *How to Marry a Millionaire*. In a chilly age of institutionalized frigidity—when a man and his wife, let alone an unwed couple, could not be shown on screen in the same bed—Marilyn Monroe was a very hot volcano.

They drove 200 miles and stopped in Paso Robles and ate steak by candle-light. A waiter asked for their autographs and they obliged, telling him they were headed for Hollywood. But they doubled back to the Clifton Motel. After making sure the rooms had television, DiMaggio paid the four-dollar nightly rate and carried his blonde bride across the threshold. They hung out a DO NOT DISTURB sign and remained in the room for fifteen hours.

Shortly after their departure the next morning for a remote cabin in the mountains above Palm Springs, the proprietor of the Clifton Motel, a savvy Greek immigrant named Jake Panapoulous, installed a plaque above the bed in Room 33 that stated simply: Joe and Marilyn Slept Here. The Clifton Motel had become a tourist attraction.

6

When Will Lomax floated across the carpets of Ted Mackey's office the next morning, he was delighted to see his boss reading the New York *Daily Mirror*. As soon as Will had heard about the wedding on the radio, he bought every tabloid and gossip sheet he could find. He stayed up watching the eleven o'clock news, then got up early to read the morning papers. He had never felt more ready for a day of work.

'Have a seat,' Ted said without looking up. 'Guess you heard they went ahead and got hitched.'

'Saw it on the late news last night. DiMagg must've kissed her fifty times for the cameras. Poor guy.' Ted kept reading. 'Have you got to the part yet about the Clifton Motel?'

'That's what I'm reading now. Jesus.'

'I know. Fifteen hours.'

'Sounds like she wore him out.'

'Or vice versa. I guess DiMagg swings a pretty big bat in the bedroom.' Will had rehearsed the line all morning. But Ted simply grunted.

Will started to stand, but Ted motioned for him to remain seated. 'We got our first two-week sales figures this morning,' he said.

'How do they look?'

'Good. Better than good. We moved well over ten thousand units in each of the first two weeks of the year. You know what that means, don't you?'

'Ummm . . .'

'Come on, come on. What's our sales goal for '54?'

'Half a million.'

'Ten thousand units a week for fifty-two weeks equals?'

'Let's see. Five hundred and twenty thousand?'

'Bravo.' The dark eyes focused hard on Will, made him feel hot and small. Ted leaned forward. 'We can do it, Will. We can beat Plymouth! People are already talking about how much iron we're moving. The power's in those numbers now, and if we beat Plymouth I promise you some people around here will be going

places. That includes you.' Will had no idea what to say. Ted clapped his hands. 'So quit sitting there. Get to work.'

The sound of Ted Mackey's secretary squawked over the box: 'Ned Schroeder on line three. He says it's important.'

'I'd better take that,' Ted said. 'It could be about Marilyn.'

7

On his way up the White House driveway to watch the President and First Lady board the helicopter that would take them to Camp David for the weekend, Morey Caan spotted a man with close-cropped hair sitting alone on the South Lawn. He was wearing a trench coat and studying the trees. Morey stopped and stared. 'Holy shit,' he whispered. It was Pete Hoover, a classmate and fellow history major at the University of Virginia, now a CIA agent, the star of last year's *coup* that brought the Shah of Iran back to power—and one of Morey's most prized sources. What the hell was Pete Hoover doing on the South Lawn staring at the trees? Morey was about to call out to him when he heard the familiar braying of the reporters. He sprinted up the driveway and arrived just as Mamie ducked into the helicopter. Ike stood on the grass smiling as cameras clicked and reporters shouted their questions, babble so familiar to Morey that he barely heard it any more: 'Planning to speak out against Senator McCarthy? . . . Chinchilla coat? . . . Chance to play golf?' Then the President raised his hand and there was silence. Ike cleared his throat. 'Mamie and I,' he said, 'both think they make a lovely couple and wish them all the best.' He stepped into the helicopter and rose into the sky.

After scribbling the quote in his notebook, Morey turned to the nearest reporter, lanky Russell Baker of the *New York Times*: 'Who was he talking about?'

'Julius and Ethel Rosenberg,' Baker said.

'Very funny, Russ.'

'He was talking about DiMaggio and Monroe, dummy,' said mustachioed Mary Messina, 225 pounds worth of Associated Press correspondent. 'Come on, Morey. You know that Joe and

Marilyn are more important to Ike than our silly-assed questions about McCarthy.'

There was much grumbling as the reporters and photographers shuffled down the driveway. Ike's departure had generated no news, and that meant there would be no stories to file, no photographs to process. It was time to start drinking.

'The first round's on me,' Mary announced.

This was greeted with cheers. Morey had rushed here for one lousy quote that wasn't even good enough to use in *Straight from the Horse's Mouth.*

8

Claire Hathaway had come to hate her sketches of the 1957 tail-lights. They reminded her of gargoyles. The lights were set in backward-slanting slabs of chrome, fat wedges of shiny silver metal that rose to sharp points, as though they'd been sculpted by the wind and the forward velocity of the car. But there was so much chrome around the lights Claire wondered how a mere car would be able to support the weight. In any event, that would be a problem for the boys in engineering. She had heard a rumor that the '57 Cadillacs and Chevys had already sprouted fins. *Fins*!

'Verrry nice.'

She spun on her stool, startled. 'Mr Mackey. You scared me half to death.'

He was standing inside her cubicle with his PR man. They were dressed in charcoal-gray suits, their shoes blazing black. They looked like bankers, or undertakers. Ted leaned over her drawing board. 'These must be the tail-lights for the '57.'

'Yes. And they're giving me fits.'

'Well, I think they're very nice.'

He was so close she could smell him—talcum powder and shaving-lotion, a strange salt-water scent. The silver hair was swept back. The collar of his white shirt was stiff with starch. He looked at his PR flack. 'Will, could you give us a minute alone?'

Opposite: Dwight D. Eisenhower

Will Lomax drifted out of the studio. Claire wiggled her feet back into her brown penny loafers.

'I've been meaning to tell you how happy everyone is with the front end of the new Century,' Ted said. 'The dealers love it. We moved more than ten thousand units last week, and that front end is a big selling point.'

'Thanks, but a dozen of us worked on the front end, you know.'

'I know,' Ted Mackey said and looked over his shoulder. He saw the members of the Buick studio toiling over sketches of tail-lights, dashboards, hub-caps, bumpers. He looked down at Claire. 'Let's take a little walk.'

They stepped out into the hall, and Ted Mackey clasped his hands behind his back. 'Let me get right to the point, Claire. I've got a problem and I need your help. I don't want you to breathe a word about this to anyone.' He lowered his voice. 'We think someone in this studio might be leaking our designs to the competition. I don't need to tell you how serious this could be. If you don't mind, I'd like to talk to you about it. In private.'

'You don't think I would—'

He chuckled. 'You're not a suspect, for God's sake. That's why I need to talk to you. Over dinner. Is Monday night good for you?'

'Umm . . .'

'Strictly business.'

'Gee, I—these sketches are due first thing Tuesday morning. Is there any way I can get a rain-check?'

'Not if you want to have a job on Tuesday.'

'Well, in that case my answer is yes.'

'A wise decision. Eight o'clock Monday night at the Detroit Club.'

She strolled back to the studio alone. When she tried to return to work on her sketch, she found she couldn't concentrate. She kept thinking of their kiss at the New Year's Eve party and of his remark—'strictly business'—and she had the uneasy feeling that a man in his position would offer such a reassurance only if he had something quite different from business in mind.

9

The snow began to stick just as Will Lomax started home. He narrowly missed the cars in front, both having corkscrewed into a ditch, and negotiated the treacherous turn from Plymouth Road on to Southfield Road, gripping the Buick Century's basketball hoop-sized steering-wheel and easing the car toward the suburbs. At Eight Mile Road he skidded to a stop at the light, the Detroit city limit, the birth of the suburbs.

The snow was coming out of the north, falling faster, a blur in the headlights. This kind of snow could fall for days, with drifts piling up to the windows of his house, then up to the roof. Will thought of the two towering magnolia trees in the front yard of his boyhood home in Virginia. He had seen them covered with snow just twice, and the snow had looked like sugar. This snow did not.

Will settled into the line of crawling cars. He could see that the conversation he had had with Morey had set the tone for the entire rotten day. When Will confessed that he'd been so busy he hadn't given a thought to *The Book*, Morey had snapped, 'So what's the matter? You already forget about your trip to Washington last year?'

Of course Will hadn't forgotten.

He had been summoned to Washington to assist in a delicate operation: the confirmation hearings before the hostile Senate Armed Services Committee of President-elect Eisenhower's nominee for Secretary of Defense, former GM president Charles ('Engine Charlie') Wilson, one of the richest of the very rich men who had been tapped for a Cabinet that was already being called 'the Millionaires' Club'.

Will was chosen because he had worked as a newspaper reporter on Capitol Hill and was seen as the perfect tutor to teach the nominee how to deal with the Washington press corps, a group Wilson referred to as 'those pricks'. And Will, like most members of the Armed Services Committee itself, was a southerner.

Will arrived on a rainy January afternoon in 1953 and went

straight up to the GM suite on the top floor of the Shoreham Hotel, where he spent two days with Charlie Wilson and a small army of blue-suits—White House liaisons, Congressional aides, secret service men, representatives from the GM Salary and Bonus Committee, corporate lawyers, GOP lawyers, Washington lawyers, tax lawyers. Most of the fuss was over what Charlie Wilson would do with his vast GM stock and his bonuses now that he could direct millions of dollars of business GM's way.

When the hearings began, things turned sour almost immediately. The culprit was the senator from Texas, Lyndon Johnson. Johnson asked if Wilson had any documents to offer the Committee. Wilson handed over his letters of resignation from oil companies, banks and boards along with a document outlining the cash and the 1,737 shares of GM stock bonuses due him over the next four years.

'And what do you intend to do with that cash and those stocks as they become available to you?' Johnson asked.

'Why, I intend to keep them.'

A ripple passed through the press gallery. 'What is the value of that stock, the par value?' Johnson asked.

'The par value is five dollars,' Wilson said. 'The market value is about sixty-five or sixty-six dollars, something like that. Some of you probably have some. I doubt if I'm the only man in this room who has any.'

'Well, I do not have any,' Johnson said, pausing for effect. 'And if I did, I would know what it's worth.'

Snickers from the press gallery. Wilson bit his lip and then fielded a few innocuous questions from Senator Leverett Saltonstall. Then it was the turn of Senator Robert Hendrickson, a Republican trench warrior from New Jersey. 'Mr Wilson,' he said, 'I am interested to know whether—if a situation did arise where you had to make a decision that was adverse to the interest of your stock in General Motors—could you make that decision?'

'Yessir, I could,' Wilson said firmly. 'But I cannot conceive of such a situation because for years I thought that what was good for the country was good for General Motors—and vice versa. The difference did not exist. Our company is too big and powerful. It goes with the welfare of the country. Our contribution to the nation is quite considerable.'

The pencils in the press gallery were racing. What a gem! *What's good for the country is good for General Motors.* Engine Charlie Wilson had just made Washington headlines.

And now, a year after his Washington trip, Will Lomax had been promoted to the top PR job at Buick and was driving a company car into another blizzard and felt utterly, blackly lost.

He guided the Buick off Southfield Road into his driveway. A foot of snow had already fallen but the white frame house was warm when he got inside, miraculously warm and quiet. After a day of telephones, meetings, arguments, traffic and snow, the deep warm silence seemed magical. He stood in the kitchen and listened: only the faint ticking of the grandfather clock in the foyer and the faraway murmuring of a television set.

He filled a tall glass with ice cubes and Old Crow, and as he poured he noticed a new appliance beside its box on the counter top—a Hurrie-Hot Electri-Cup. It had a removeable egg rack and, he discovered on reading the instructions, it could boil twenty-three ounces of liquid, plus baby bottles, instant coffee and eggs. It cost $14.95. It looked like a stainless steel toadstool. Next to it was an unopened box. Will looked inside: it was a device called the Power-Chef Mixer. There were mixing bowls, a juice strainer and a ten-speed mixer that doubled as a meat grinder. The other day Margaret had suggested that winter was the perfect time to buy an air-conditioner for their bedroom window, and she happened to have found a Westinghouse model for less than $400. Hurrie-Hots, Electri-Cups, Power-Chefs, air-conditioners, TV dinners and color TV.

10

Morey Caan was frantic. He was running late for his interview with Senator McCarthy and knew that the only thing the Great Red Hunter hated more than a Commie in the State Department was a reporter who kept him waiting. As Morey fumbled with the key to lock his apartment, the phone rang inside. He unlocked the door and raced back in.

'Morey! Pete Hoover here, returning your call. How the hell you be?'

'Pete, I was just on my way out.'

'Got a message you tried to reach me. What's up?' There was a rustling sound, then a muffled: 'Go fuck yerselves.'

'Come again?'

'Nothing. These pricks playing poker in the back think they own the joint. Fuck 'em.'

'Where are you, Pete?'

'Bill's Grille—home of the world's tastiest Gibson.'

Bill's Grille was a grim, smoky little hole in the wall. When Morey worked for the *Post* he dropped in there two or three times a week to peruse the local rummies, retired military boys, Pentagon paper pushers and the occasional disgruntled spook like Pete Hoover.

'The reason I called before, Pete, was to see what you were doing on the South Lawn the other day.'

'Jeez, you crazy little bug-eyed bastard, you don't miss a trick, do you?' He coughed. Then he sighed. 'Aww, what the hell. Y'aren't gonna believe this one.'

'Try me.' Morey took out a notebook and pen.

'About a month ago the Agency assigned me to the White House and told me to shoot the fucking squirrels.'

'Did you say shoot the *squirrels*?'

'Shoot the *fucking* squirrels is what I said. They've got me shooting the fucking squirrels!'

'Why?'

'Last year the American Public Golf Association built a putting-green for Ike on the South Lawn so that he could keep his short game sharp and all that shit. And he loves it. But there's a small problem.'

'Fucking squirrels.'

'Bingo. See, when Truman was in the White House he liked to feed the squirrels, so by the time he left town the little fuckers were so fat and sassy they would eat right out of your hand. Now they bury their nuts in Ike's new putting-green. About a month ago his perfect putt hit a bump and bounced wide and Ike blew a gasket and told his butler, this little Filipino fag named Moaney, to shoot the next squirrel he saw. Moaney contacted the Secret Service and the Secret Service contacted the FBI and the FBI contacted the Agency. Squirrel duty, my bosses decided, would be just the thing for me.'

Morey didn't know what to say. Even by American standards, going from the cutting-edge of international espionage in Iran to squirrel-shooting duty on the White House lawn was an astonishingly swift fall from grace. And which was worse—a President who loved animals but had it in him to drop two atomic bombs, or a President who loved golf but had it in him to shoot squirrels for fucking up his putting-green?

'Pete, I'd like to get together and talk more about this, but right now I've got to get down to the Hill for an interview.'

'I'm here every afternoon from five o'clock on. Corner barstool.'

11

When her husband phoned to say he wouldn't be home for dinner—something about having to take some salesmen out on the town—Milmary Mackey was sitting at the kitchen table studying the snapshot she'd dug out of the attic on New Year's Eve. It was a picture of a young pilot, a dark-haired, athletic man, sprinting toward the camera. A gray airplane, its nose in the dirt and its twin tails in the air, burned in the distance. Ever since she showed it to Harvey Pearl on New Year's Day, the snapshot had been in her mind. She even dreamed about it. And now at the age of thirty-six, in the dead middle of a winter day, in the dead middle of her life, Milmary sensed that solving the riddles inside this snapshot offered a chance of salvation from a life that had become an endless cycle of cocktail parties, hangovers, Garden Club meetings, bridge games, station-wagon rides with her sons, cookouts and requests to canvass door-to-door to help fight tuberculosis, diabetes, heart disease, cancer and gout.

Photo: Eve Arnold/Magnum

She stared at the snapshot. The startling thing about it, she realized, was that the man's face gave no indication that he was in danger or afraid. The face had the glad abandon of a boy's. He could have been dashing down a beach or a football field instead of running from a crippled, burning airplane, a plume of smoke curling from the cockpit into the sky. The gray of that sky reminded Milmary of how it had actually looked— grainy and evil and hot. The memory made her shiver. She hadn't felt that sensation in years, not since the 1930s when she fled Detroit and entered the humid little New York world of writers and radicals and painters and poets. Compared to provincial Detroit, it was exotic and exhilarating and full of raffish characters, who all came to refer to Milmary Cavanagh as 'the virgin'.

The label was not flattering. She was fresh out of the University of Michigan and had published her first short story in *Collier's*. Her talent may have been unformed, even ordinary, but her looks were not. Everyone wanted to bed the Irish beauty with the auburn hair and the long legs, and the reputation for having turned her back on a vast fortune somewhere in the Midwest in order to pursue her writing career. And just about everyone tried to bed her. But they all, to a man, failed.

She had enough talent to make the fawning of established writers credible, and she was naïve enough at first to believe they invited her to their parties and up to their shabby apartments to discuss the finer points of dialogue and plot. It became a kind of game to see who would be the first to break through. No less a heavyweight than Eugene O'Neill gave it his best shot. After taking Milmary to see *Mourning Becomes Elektra*, he got her up to his apartment, plied her with theater talk and red wine, actually unbuttoned her blouse—then watched in horror as she sprang from the sofa, buttoned up her blouse again, smoothed her hair and vanished into the Greenwich Village night. O'Neill went straight for the whisky in the kitchen. Three quick shots and he was off on an epic spree, a bout that lasted three days and nights and left him face-down, cold as an iced fish, on the Fifth Avenue trolley tracks. He was dragged to safety by a passing pedestrian. Six months later he was awarded the Nobel Prize for

Literature.

There were similar scenarios, with less grandiose finales. She was forever breaking hearts by making herself seem available. 'The virgin' was downgraded to 'the tease'. She sold a short story to the *New Yorker*, but her pile of rejection slips grew taller and she had to go to work as a proof-reader of encyclopaedias. The romance of New York was wearing thin. Like many Americans she was rescued from purgatory—in her case not a purgatory of breadlines and relief checks, but one of drunken parties, dull poetry readings, rejection slips and pushy men—by the bombing of Pearl Harbor. Her father got her a job writing press releases and publicity copy for General Motors' new War Production Office, and so, feeling like that most pulverized of American fauna, the failed writer, she left New York in the spring of 1942 and moved into an apartment building her father owned in Windsor, Ontario. She didn't have to pay rent and had a sweeping view of downtown Detroit across the river.

But she was lonely and miserable. One of her first assignments was to write a pamphlet about the Wildcat fighter plane GM was building for the Navy. And then, to her delight, the more she learned the more she wanted to know. She was surprised to discover that American planes were inferior to the enemy's, particularly the Japanese Zero and the German Messerschmitt, but was equally surprised, if not horrified, to see how feverishly American industry was determined to catch up: everyone was committed to designing and building better, faster, deadlier warplanes. It had become a national obsession. So many companies were involved—GM, Grumman, Northrop, Lockheed, North American, Boeing, Bell, Chrysler and dozens of others— and they were cranking out bullets, Jeeps, tanks, cannons, land-mines, rockets, machine-guns, battleships, aircraft-carriers, submarines and bombs, always more bombs, you couldn't have too many bombs. She was beginning to comprehend the true power of America and the madness of the war.

Her first interview for the Wildcat pamphlet was with the head of all the design teams working on GM's defense contracts. From his imposing title and rich voice on the telephone, she had expected someone big and solid, and dressed in a uniform. What she found behind an unmarked door was a man barely five feet tall with a flat-top haircut, suspenders and bow-tie. His moustache looked like a frayed whisk broom.

'Harvey Pearl?' she said, shaking his hand.

'No, actually I'm Clark Gable. This is a disguise.'

Harvey led her to his studio, a large, white, sky-lit room. The walls were covered with meticulous sketches and blueprints of an airplane.

'So this,' she said, pointing to one of the drawings, 'is the mighty Wildcat?'

'No. The Wildcat's history as far as we're concerned. It's in production at our plant in Linden, New Jersey,' Harvey said and started rummaging in a box under his drawing table. He dug out a photograph of a single-seat, twin-engine plane with twin tail booms.

'Now this,' Harvey said softly, 'is a true work of art. The Lockheed Lightning, the P-38, an absolute masterpiece of design.'

'It's . . . pretty.'

'She's *beautiful*. Compared to her, these other things we're cranking out are dogs. He gazed at the picture as though it were of a lovely woman. He whispered, '*Der Gabelschwanz Teufel*.'

'*Der* what?'

'*Der Gabelschwanz Teufel*. The Fork-Tailed Devil. If you happened to work for the German Luftwaffe these days, that's what you'd call her. I suspect she's going to do even better in the Pacific.' He snapped his fingers. 'I've got an idea! They're training to fly the P-38 up at Selfridge, not far from here. We could drive up tomorrow and see the plane in action and you could interview a GM employee who's training to be a pilot. Trust me, it'll make a much better story than the Wildcat.'

They left early the next morning in Harvey's yellow and green 1927 Cadillac La Salle, one of his trade marks, the first car he designed. Harvey had a deep love for it. It was the car that led to one of GM's most lucrative innovations, what some called 'the annual model change' and others the 'planned obsolescence'. Harvey didn't care what people called it. It had made engineers subservient to stylists; it had become an American institution, and it had made him a very rich and powerful man.

Milmary Cavanagh loved the car for different reasons: for the purr of the big V-8 engine and the way people looked at them when they drove past. She also loved the plush leather seats; they smelled like money.

Selfridge Field turned out to be a platter of dirt surrounded by scruffy pine trees, Quonset huts, barracks, hangars and a single forlorn wind-sock. Harvey Pearl parked in the shade near the radio shack and lowered the top. To Milmary, everything looked dry and dusty. Even the P-38s, so sleek and dazzling in the photograph, looked drab as they rolled out of the hangars. The only bright touches had been provided by the pilots who, like most men about to go off to war, had developed a fondness bordering on physical love for their instruments of death and had painted terms of endearment near the machine-guns in the nose-cones: 'Miss Virginia', 'Stinky 2', 'L'il'. The last plane that thundered past had nothing painted on its nose-cone. It lifted into the sky and banked over the trees by the lake.

'That's our boy,' Harvey said.

By the time it reappeared, a breeze had sprung up and the wind-sock was horizontal. Sand skittered across the airstrip. Through a pair of binoculars, Harvey studied the planes as they returned. Milmary thought they looked awkward as they touched down, twisting and bouncing, a sharp change from their effortless departures.

'That breeze is fooling them,' Harvey said. He focused the binoculars on the final plane coming in over the trees. 'Easy boy, easy. Keep your nose up. I said *up*, dammit, *keep the nose up!*'

The plane hit the ground hard, bounced once, then slammed down with such force that the landing-gear under the nose-cone buckled. Both propellers snapped off, spraying metal, and the plane went into a nose-first skid. Sparks showered the cockpit. The plane came to rest just short of the fence; a fire truck appeared from one of the Quonset huts and raced down the airstrip. The plane started to burn. The cockpit opened, and the pilot popped out, slid down the wing and hit the ground sprinting. When the fuel tank exploded he was knocked down, but got up and kept running.

Harvey stood on the Cadillac's front seat, snapped three pictures and then joined the pilots and mechanics hurrying out to meet the pilot.

Harvey guided the pilot over toward the Cadillac. Even in his lumpy flight suit he was solidly built, an athlete; he had thick wrists and broad shoulders. Standing next to Harvey, he looked like a giant. He was holding a kerchief to his nose and was bleeding badly.

'Milmary Cavanagh,' Harvey said, 'this is Ted Mackey. Maybe we should come back tomorrow for that interview. Ted now has to report to his commanding officer.'

He smiled. He had perfect teeth to go with an oft-broken nose.

'Or maybe Ted comes to Detroit from time to time,' Milmary said.

'Every chance I get.'

'Wonderful. I'll buy you dinner Saturday night at the Detroit Club. Upstairs dining-room at eight o'clock.'

Harvey and Milmary drove off but stopped near the charred P-38 and shut off the engine. The plane looked like it was trying to bury its nose in the dirt, a great crippled insect. 'He's a lucky man,' Harvey said.

For the rest of that brutally hot summer, Ted Mackey spent his weekdays at Selfridge Field mastering the P-38 and his weekends in Detroit pursuing Milmary Cavanagh. After his crash, he seemed to lose all fear and became the hottest jock in the 1st Pursuit Group, able to coax the plane into the steepest dives and hold on just a little longer than the other pilots before pulling out and soaring up to cruising altitude. It was this daring maneuver, which he executed to perfection, that would help write the legend of the P-38 in the Pacific.

Ted took Milmary to Belle Isle for boat rides, to Tigers games, movies, dinner, even the symphony once. At the end of every evening she gave him a handshake or a peck on the cheek, hopped into her big black Plymouth and roared away.

One night in early September when Detroit felt again like a

blast furnace, Milmary invited Ted to her apartment after they had been to the movies. It was the first time he'd set foot inside. While she fixed drinks in the kitchen, he sat on the sofa and gazed across the river at the Penobscot Building and the lesser stalagmites of downtown Detroit. Ships, loaded with raw materials or finished weapons, slid back and forth on the black water. He had news to tell her.

'*Voilà!*' Milmary set down on the coffee-table a silver tray with a shaker and two glasses and a bowl of green olives and two brimming glasses.

They clinked glasses and drank. She turned off the lights and sat beside him. They sipped their drinks in silence and watched the lights of downtown and the Ambassador Bridge and the passing ships. When his glass was empty, Ted cleared his throat. 'Milmary, there's—'

'Wait! You haven't eaten your olive yet. It's the best part.'

She popped the olive into his mouth. When he bit into it, there was an explosion, a delicious blaze on his tongue.

'I soaked them in gin. Just for you.'

She placed fresh olives in the glasses and refilled them. Then she stood up and held out her hand. 'Come with me.'

He was lifted off the sofa and led down a dark hallway to a large white sugar cube of a bed; it glowed in the reflected river lights. He felt confused; there was a riot inside his skull. She took his glass and set it beside hers on the night table; then she pulled him down on to her.

Once, later, as he fumbled for cigarettes on the night table, she said, 'Do you always smoke after sex?'

'I don't know. I never looked.'

It took her a moment to catch the joke, and when she did she laughed a deep laugh, racking and ragged. A new humming bundle of nerves had been awakened inside her, and, lying there, sticky and fragrant, she realized that she had surrendered something precious, something she had been saving all her life, and that now she would be repaid.

When he stubbed his cigarette in the ashtray, she ran her fingers through his dark, sweaty hair. He sounded very far away when he said, 'Our orders came today.'

'Your what?'

'Our orders. We ship out for New Guinea tomorrow. I wanted to tell you earlier . . .'

After a long silence, she said, 'Somehow I knew.'

'Make me a promise,' she then said.

'Anything.'

'Promise me you won't get yourself killed—and that you'll come back for me.'

Milmary awoke late, sore, alone and afraid—that she was pregnant, that he would never come back, that she would be disowned by her family. But three weeks later her period arrived along with the first of many letters from Ted Mackey. 'My darling Mil,' the letter began, 'we had our first contact with Japanese Zeroes this morning . . .' She'd been so scared and lonely she had forgotten the danger he was in.

She received that first letter two weeks after it was written. At the very moment she was reading it, a young Japanese pilot, Flight Petty Officer Toshiki Ishihara, was on the flight deck of the aircraft-carrier *Ryujo*, anchored half-way around the world just north of the Admiralty Islands, virtually on the equator. This would have been the day that Toshiki Ishihara had been waiting for, the day he would fly his first combat mission in a Zero-sen, the new Mitsubishi A6M2 Model 21 fighter, the pride of the Japanese Navy. But he wouldn't live to see the end. This would also be the day that Ted Mackey would shoot down his first Zero.

Ted Mackey was the sudden hero of the 1st Pursuit Group, but didn't bask in his glory long. Two months later, on the day he downed his third Zero, his left engine overheated and caught fire. He limped along with one engine, escorted by Major Richard Bong, who, on his way to racking up forty kills, saved Ted's life by chasing away the two Zeroes that descended on his crippled P-38 with 'Mil' painted in bright red letters on its nose-cone. By the time Ted reached the airstrip, the heat inside the cockpit was so fierce he could barely hold the control wheel. He came in too fast and the right landing-gear snapped, sending the plane into a corkscrewing skid—a maneuver, he joked later, that he had perfected at Selfridge Field. He was pulled from the plane unconscious, his left kneecap shattered, his left foot badly burned. After flying fifty-two combat missions, downing three enemy planes and being awarded the Distinguished Service Cross and the Purple Heart, Lieutenant Ted Mackey was on his way home to Detroit.

Ted Mackey and Milmary Cavanagh were married in Detroit Cathedral on New Year's Day 1943.

On one side of the aisle were Ted's people, the shanty Irish, his gimp-legged father, his stout doughy mother, his siblings and in-laws and their litters, a badly done-up gang of wage slaves, union men, wife beaters, boozers and juvenile delinquents. On the other side were Milmary's people, the lace Irish fresh from the salons of Grosse Pointe: blue-haired dowagers, tycoons, debutantes and politicos—well tailored, heavily perfumed, lavishly coiffed and brutally barbered.

William Cavanagh had made no secret of his displeasure with his daughter's choice of a mate. 'He just won't do,' he kept telling her and even mentioned his will. Though he didn't admit it, William Cavanagh would have been secretly afraid that Ted Mackey was after his money. But his fears were groundless. Ted wanted to make his own money and acquire his own power—not the abstract, ward-heeler variety, but the kind that existed at General Motors, power you could feel and smell, the power to boss thousands of people in the world's largest industrial empire.

In the end, the family's objections didn't matter. Milmary would do what she would do, as she had always done all her life.

Now, ten years later, sitting at the kitchen table in the big white house on Mirror Lake, the mother of two boys—the wife of a man who had made good and was determined to make even better—Milmary Mackey wondered what to do about a snapshot that was like a taunt, a nasty reminder that she had given up too easily her dream of being a writer and had settled for too little in life.

She put the picture of the sprinting pilot and the burning plane back in the box. She watched the children skating on the lake. She was terrified, and her hands were trembling.

12

Claire Hathaway awoke at seven o'clock the next morning with a jackhammer knocking inside her skull. The pain was hot and angry, and her mouth tasted like a squirrel had crawled into it and died. She didn't dare move.

She opened her eyes and saw the picture of the 1954 Buick on the wall at the foot of her bed. It had a creamy yellow body and a white top and a flaming red interior. It was the first '54 Buick to roll off the Flint assembly line, and she had to admit it was a stunning departure from the stodgy cars of the '40s and early '50s, one that declared that the war was history and that times were good. The car was sleek and low-slung—two of Harvey Pearl's prime objectives—and looked as though it were in motion even when parked. Yes, that was what made Claire proud of the '54 Buick Century: it looked like it was always in motion.

The '57s would be different. She had been told late in the afternoon that she was to complete the tail-light sketches for a design review this morning, but what could she have said? 'Sorry, I got a dinner date with Ted Mackey.' So she hadn't left the Tech Center until after eight o'clock, and by the time she reached the brownstone fortress of the Detroit Club, she was so nervous she sat with the engine idling and debated whether to get out or drive home. Inside it was worse. Bevelled mirrors fractured the light, and every time she turned she was confronted with herself. Her hair looked awful. After trying to do something with it in the ladies' room, she paused outside the library and watched the old men in high-backed red leather chairs smoking cigars and reading newspapers on bamboo sticks, studying the stock quotations.

Upstairs the *maître d'* smiled and bowed. She could feel every eye in the room on her as she followed him to the far corner, where Ted Mackey was sitting in with a single candle burning and a *Wall Street Journal*. He stubbed out his cigarette and stood up. She was so uneasy she ordered an Old-Fashioned from the *maître d'* before she sat down. Ted didn't object. In fact, by the time she finished her second drink, he was well into his fourth.

He ordered an expensive bottle of French burgundy and drank most of it as he told her about growing up poor in Detroit. As he talked she remembered one of her mother's truths about men: they are their own favorite topics of conversation. He loved telling his story, and some of its details came back to her now: the night he fought Amos Fuller's father for the city Golden Gloves title and was so scared he vomited on his father's back, leaving the ring; the legendary arm of Chick Hewitt, who could throw a rock and make a seagull explode in mid-air; the neighborhood pastime of lobbing bricks over the fence of the Cadillac plant on Michigan Avenue; the night a bloated Negro corpse washed up on the beach at Belle Isle.

As his story unfolded, Claire realized that nothing in her childhood matched the glamor and struggle and sheer action of his. What could she come back with? The way a girl's reputation in Ames, Iowa, was ruined if her date stopped for gas at the Hudson station because everyone knew there was a condom machine in the men's room? Or a typical night drinking Cokes and eating pork tenderloin sandwiches at the Rainbow Café? Cruising the Dairy Dreme and the Ranch Drive-In? Nothing in Ames ever exploded, shattered or washed ashore.

Claire sat up in bed. She couldn't possibly make it to work—but couldn't call in sick because she had to review the '57 tail-light sketches. She shuffled into the bathroom, turned on the shower and swallowed four aspirins that came right back up but that two glasses of water then forced down. Standing very still under the stream of hot water, she remembered Ted asking her if she thought the stylists she'd worked with on the '54 Century were loyal to the company. What a strange question. He sounded like Joe McCarthy. What did *loyalty* have to do with designing cars? He had leaned forward as he asked the question, his face close to hers, warm and orange in the candlelight, the wiry eyebrows dancing. Those eyes, so full of mischief, reminded her of another thing her mother had tried to teach her about men: don't trust them.

Claire had always ignored this piece of motherly advice because its origin was so obvious. What woman whose husband had gone to the corner for a pack of cigarettes and never come back *wouldn't* warn her daughter to beware of the devils?

While other girls became cheerleaders, Claire grew up hanging around the garage of their next-door neighbor, an eccentric sports car buff named Don Chadwick who worked at the Synchrotron, a clump of gray buildings on the edge of town where men in white coats smashed atoms for a living. She helped him take a British MG-TC apart bolt by bolt and put it back together, and as payment he taught her how to drive—on a stick shift with the steering-wheel on the right side. Nothing in her life had come close to the sensation of sailing down a country road in that green MG with the top down and Mr Chadwick at her side in his snap-brim cap, the cornfields whipping past and the road unfurling ahead of them forever.

Soon she was designing her own cars and, while other girls were dreaming of getting some boy's ID bracelet, she was rebuilding a 1939 Buick she'd bought from a chicken farmer for twenty-five dollars.

No boy had the nerve to ask her out. She felt the same scorn for high school boys she'd always felt for high school girls: the boys seemed to worry only about sports and cars, which weren't much better than shopping and hair. To escape she started devouring the fat novels her mother assigned to her students—*Crime and Punishment* and *Jane Eyre* and *Madame Bovary*.

During the Christmas vacation of her senior year, she went out with Charlie Craig, a class-mate of her brother's who was home from Cornell for the holidays. They went to the Rainbow Café and ordered pork tenderloin sandwiches and talked about *Madame Bovary* for three hours. Claire was elated. Besides her mother, he was the first person she'd met who had even heard of the book. Charlie Craig had just read it for a literature course at Cornell taught by a crazy Russian who collected butterflies in his spare time and wrote obscure novels. Then and there Claire decided she had to meet this man who could make Emma Bovary's plight so compelling to his students. But when she announced she wanted to go to Cornell in the fall, her mother said, 'You're being impetuous again. We have a perfectly good college right here in town.' And that settled it. She would go to

Cornell and find this Russian named Vladimir Nabokov.

The shower began to go cold. She shut it off and the telephone was ringing. Wrapped in a towel, dripping and shivering, she picked up the receiver in the living-room. 'Hello?'

'Did I wake you up?'

'Mr Mackey! No, I was just getting out of the shower.'

'It's *Ted*, remember? How you feeling?'

'God-awful. I just ate a whole bottle of aspirin. What on earth did we drink last night, battery acid?'

He was chuckling. 'I'm in pretty rough shape myself. So tell me, what did you decide about lunch?'

'Lunch?'

'You promised me you'd let me buy you lunch this week.'

'Oh, right.'

'How does Friday sound?'

'Fine, I guess.'

'This time you get to do all the talking. And please give some thought to the other thing we discussed.'

'What other thing?'

'The people you worked with on the '54, particularly the front end—you know, whether or not you think they can be trusted.'

'Oh, that.'

'You will give it some thought, won't you?'

'Sure, I'll try.'

'Don't try, Claire. Do it.'

There was a thrilling edge to the command. 'OK,' she said, 'I'll do it.'

13

Jews were not ordinarily welcome at the National Presbyterian Church, but then Morey Caan—carrying a borrowed Bible and wearing a clean necktie, a white shirt and a dark suit—was not an ordinary Jew.

He breezed in early one Sunday morning and took a seat about ten pews behind the roped-off presidential section.

He was always impressed by how successful the high Protestants were at bleeding the color and passion from their churches. He once visited a Congregational church in Vermont and thought he was in a hospital operating-room. Morey supposed Ike chose this particular church because it was appropriately both grand and bland, all sandstone and granite and frosted windows, no marble or stained glass or clouds of incense or wild singing. No nothing. Just right for Ike and Mamie.

Morey knew that Ike had never once attended church and that he'd joined a church in Washington only because he felt it was important for the President to set a good example. The denomination didn't matter to Ike. God wasn't what brought him here every Sunday.

Morey pretended to read the *Book of Ecclesiastes* and tried to remember if Truman had also gone to church. It was an intriguing question. He could imagine Truman not having much use for man-made religion and not bothering to pretend he did. That was one thing Morey liked about Truman. He was the butt of a lot of jokes, but at least he did what he thought was right and never apologized and never looked back. Morey doubted Truman ever lost sleep over Hiroshima and Nagasaki.

There was a rustling at the back of the church. Morey turned and watched as Ike and Mamie came strolling up the aisle. Even these rock-ribbed Presbyterians turned and gawked. When the Eisenhowers reached the front pew, Mamie paused to acknowledge the people sitting nearby. Morey thought she looked a bit puffy, but then remembered that Sunday was the only day she rolled out of bed before noon.

The service was more boring than the building and the people in it, and Morey dozed off. When he awoke everyone was standing and singing a hymn. He slipped outside to get in position for the presidential exit.

Out front, the Secret Service boys gave Morey a good raking with their eyes. He pretended to admire the sunny morning and was careful to keep his back to the reporters and photographers roped off on the far side of Ike's limousine. He heard the familiar rustling and turned just as Ike and Mamie came through the doors, down the steps and into the sunshine. They chatted with their fellow Presbyterians, smiled, gave the photographers an opportunity to snap a few pictures. Morey eased into the crowd of church-goers and worked his way up close. It would be so easy to kill him, Morey thought.

Half a dozen people were talking at once to Ike and Mamie, and they both stood there beaming, nodding, not saying a word. Then Ike held out his arm and said, 'Dear, we have to run along now.'

Mamie sighed as though this was the worst news she'd heard in a week. Then, to a woman in a mink stole with a blue cloud of cotton-candy hair, she said: 'You should tell him what I told him when he asked *me* that question.'

'What was that?' the woman said.

'I said, "Mr Pearson, I *do* have a job. I have a full-time job—and his name is Ike."'

Christ, Morey thought, what a way to make a buck. There was a ripple of adoring laughter as Mamie and her full-time job disappeared into the limousine. Walking away from the church Morey jotted the quote in the notebook.

14

Before she left the Tech Center to meet Ted Mackey for lunch, Claire Hathaway spent half an hour in the ladies' room—not the little closet behind the design studio added for the three women stylists, but the plush lounge off the reception area where the secretaries and typists spent their coffee-breaks smoking cigarettes, chewing gum, gossiping and primping in front of the tall mirrors. Claire had brought make-up.

Driving south she had the uneasy feeling she was losing control. Even her '39 Buick, which had been running rough, sailed down Jefferson so fast she had to keep hitting the brakes. When she reached Grosse Pointe, the houses were large and set apart and done up like wedding-cakes and castles. She was sure Ted had suggested meeting here because it was far from the usual corporate and Tech Center spots. The Country Club of Detroit's

fairways were blanketed with snow. The clubhouse, a clump of
bricks tricked up in the Tudor style to resemble a British manor,
seemed to her a weirdly appropriate play-pen for a bunch of car
tycoons who would always have more money than taste.
Professor Nabokov, whose latest letter lay open beside her on the
front seat, would have looked at that pile of brick and exposed
timbers and tall chimneys and cried, '*Poshlost!*'

The cry would be full of both scorn and admiration, a
condemnation and an embrace of this falsely beautiful, falsely
grand monument to wealthy men's egos. That was something
Claire—and very few others—understood about Vladimir
Nabokov. Most people at Cornell assumed that since he was so
eccentric, he was a snob. Claire knew that nothing was further
from the truth. His latest letter simply reinforced what she'd
learned years ago. When she took the envelope out of the
mailbox and saw the Ithaca, New York postmark, she thought
instantly of this lunch date with Ted Mackey. Then she felt a
shiver of guilt—the first indication that she was not in control of
what she was doing. Typically, the letter was elliptical and brief:

> Claire, darling,
>
> It has been too cold to write in the Buick, but,
> undaunted, I will soon bring Lo home. Then her
> troubles will surely begin, for there are only two other
> themes I can think of that could be more repugnant to
> an American publisher: one, of course, is a Negro–
> White marriage which is a glorious success resulting in
> scores of children and grandchildren; the other, I
> suppose, is the atheist who lives a happy and useful life
> and dies in his sleep in the back seat of his Buick at the
> age of 106.
>
> Love always,
> Volodya.

The back seat of his Buick: a little reminder of that crisp
October afternoon during her freshman year when she'd finally

---

Opposite: Vladimir Nabokov in Rome

got up the nerve to accept his invitation to tea. He had been renting a Swiss-style chalet with yellow trim and jagged shingles from a professor of agriculture who was on sabbatical studying crop rotation in Java. When Claire arrived, Professor Nabokov was in the backyard, sitting in the back seat of an emerald-green 1939 Buick. It was in far worse shape than hers. It was scarred with rust, had no engine or tires and rested on four stacks of bricks. Though the lawn was neatly barbered, weeds pressed against the floorboards.

Claire stood at a distance, afraid to approach. He was sitting on the sofa-sized back seat writing on a yellow legal pad. He was wearing a dark overcoat and a white silk scarf. She was surprised by his face.

When she'd first arrived in Ithaca a month earlier, she had sought out the man who brought *Madame Bovary* to life for Charlie Craig. She first glimpsed him as he swept up the steps, overcoat and scarf flying, into the stout stone castle where he gave his legendary lectures. She had expected a dashing, athletic figure, a man who would look as comfortable on the back of a horse as in front of a typewriter. But he was soft and strangely puffy, and his face reminded her of General Douglas MacArthur without the sun-glasses and the corn-cob pipe.

He was known on campus as 'Prof Vlad' because no undergraduate seemed to know how to pronounce his name and no one dared to ask. After listening to a few of his lectures, Claire easily imagined him sensing his students' consternation and enjoying it hugely, just as he must have been delighted to learn that his popular 'Masterpieces in European Fiction' course was known as 'Dirty Lit' and his most beloved novel as 'Madame Ovary'.

She never missed a lecture. He would stand stiffly at the podium, reading from typed pages, never looking up at his rapt audience. Occasionally he would stop and take out a pencil and revise a sentence, as though he were alone in the room. She devoured every book of his available in translation.

Getting invited for tea proved easy enough once he realized she was a serious student and a fan.

His house was spectacularly ugly inside, and the hallway was crowded with gewgaws that must have come from a roadside stand on an Indian reservation—painted wooden statuettes, silver bracelets, hairy masks, stone arrowheads. Professor Nabokov settled into a lounge chair by the fireplace, and Claire sat on the sofa.

He produced a pot of tea, then launched into a monologue: about the grisly murders of two cab drivers he'd read about that day in the *New York Daily News*; the quirks of Earthquake McGoon, his favorite character in the 'L'il Abner' comic strip; the chess puzzle he'd solved that morning. He showed her a book on humming-birds and a rare specimen of butterfly, a 'painted lady', that he had netted the previous summer in Wyoming. He talked with equal ease about beetles and Buicks and Milton Berle. He compared Swiss hotels to American motels and decided he preferred the latter, especially 'tourist courts'. Finally he taught her the meaning of the Russian word *poshlost*—not only the obviously trashy, but also the falsely important, the falsely beautiful, the falsely clever and attractive. He opened an issue of *Life* to an ad for a new car and told her the photograph of the gleeful mom and dad and their kiddies jumping for joy beside their shiny new Tucker was a textbook illustration of *poshlost*.

And now, Claire thought as she hurried across the frozen parking-lot into the Country Club of Detroit, Volodya was finally about to become an American writer. His letter sounded so sunny, so full of hope. He was the last man in the world who would want to inject guilt into her life now. She was free to do as she pleased just as she—and he—had been free that October afternoon, floating above the smooth innocent lawn.

15

Ted Mackey hated to be kept waiting, especially by an employee. But this one was different. This one could get away with unheard-of things. The only question was: did she know it yet?

He sipped his coffee and looked out across the vast dining-room. Only one other table was occupied. In the far corner Henry Ford's kid brother, William Clay Ford, was drinking martinis and regaling a group of men, no doubt Ford executives, with a tale about a recent round of golf in Florida, something about a miraculous hole-in-one on a par four. The sight of a man born rich and growing effortlessly richer every day was enough to make Ted seethe with envy. He wanted to rise to the very top of General Motors, but despised the men already there, men like William Clay Ford who flaunted their inherited money and their Eastern school ties or, worse, tried to dress up their provincial Midwestern souls with such emblems of sophistication as golfing trips to Florida or a passing familiarity with opera or an exotic red Italian sports car.

'Did you want to go ahead and order, Mr Mackey?'

James Hudson, a great bullfrog of a man, one of six gold-jacketed Negro waiters who stayed on through the winter, stood above him.

'No, Hudson, but I will have some more coffee.'

As he poured the coffee, Hudson said, 'Will Mrs Mackey be joining you for lunch today?'

Ted loved the way these waiters, inner-city Negroes who'd spent long lives serving rich white folks, had developed extraordinarily sensitive social radar. They trafficked in information. It might be useful, even profitable, for Hudson to know whether the general manager of the Buick Division was having lunch with his wife, or with a Chrysler executive, or with some other woman.

'I'm waiting for one of my stylists to show up, Hudson.'

'Very good, sir.'

Ted turned and gazed out the tall windows. The sky had cleared and the golf-course sparkled as though it had been dusted with diamonds. Why was it that seeing things out of season always depressed him? A snow-blanketed golf-course, a grassy ski slope under a hot summer sun, a deserted beach pelted by icy rain—these things brought on monstrous gloom, a sense that his own life was hopelessly out of sync. It had happened the night before, when he'd gazed out different windows at a different snow-blanketed golf-course and a swimming-pool half full of ice.

He'd taken Milmary to dinner at Oakland Hills Country Club, a private act of penance for having stayed out so late with

Claire Hathaway. The evening started out as a civilized get-together of half a dozen old friends, a chance for Jack and Audrey Winters to talk about their trip to Japan, for Hank and Helen Schmidt to describe the new house they were building on Wing Lake and for Milmary to dazzle everyone with her knowledge of how Saul Bellow had written *The Adventures of Augie March*, recent winner of the National Book Award, while wandering all over Europe, staying in a cheap hotel in Paris, a castle in Salzburg, above cafés in Florence, in a room with a balcony in Rome, at the Crystal Palace Hotel in London, then in New York, Seattle, Saratoga Springs and Princeton.

'My Gawd,' Audrey Winters chirped, 'what on earth was the man writing about in all those places?'

Milmary had paused, blinked twice and said, 'Why, Chicago of course!'

Ted had laughed the loudest because he knew that none of these people had ever heard of Saul Bellow.

There hadn't been a whisper of that dreaded Detroit social staple—car talk—and Ted hadn't given a thought to design leaks, sales quotas, dealer conventions or Marilyn Monroe. But after dessert Milmary suggested the party repair to the upstairs lounge for 'a little nightcap', where she ordered a second brandy, a third, then switched to Scotch and milk, which meant that her ulcer was acting up but that she intended to get good and drunk anyway. Jack Winters stopped talking about bonsai trees and geisha girls and started in on Toyota and Nissan, which, he said, were two companies to watch out for. Ted didn't want to hear it again. The Japanese Zero had convinced him that 'made in Japan' spelled trash, and he couldn't imagine why any sane American would buy a tin can when gas was so cheap and a big, beautiful Buick so affordable.

The evening continued to slide out of control. Hank Schmidt, a Buckeye from Akron, and Leon Hirt, who had played tight end for the Michigan Wolverines, got into an argument about a clipping call in the fourth quarter of last year's Ohio State–Michigan game. Audrey Winters started crying into Ted's armpit because her eldest son had dropped out of Columbia and was running around Greenwich Village with a bunch of 'beatniks and a dope fiend.'

It was then that Ted noticed Milmary. She was dealing a hand of poker to three strangers at a corner table. The men had their jackets off, shirt-sleeves rolled up, cigars stoked. Milmary's eyelids were at half-mast. The pearls were gone from her neck. Please, he thought, let them be in her purse. She had a cigarette plugged into the corner of her mouth and was yelling at one of the Negro waiters, 'Leeroy, hon, bring me a fresh drink,' even though the man's name was Leon Trotter and she had known him for years. The woman was Jekyll and Hyde. Ted knew there was no sense trying to get her to leave. She would make a scene, embarrass him, throw her drink. In the morning, she would act as though nothing had happened.

So he positioned himself in the shadows at the far end of the bar while everyone else played poker and argued about a clipping call and fretted about their kids. He ordered a brandy and stared out at the golf course and the frozen swimming-pool.

The clubhouse was empty and quiet and Claire Hathaway felt like a trespasser.

She spotted Ted Mackey on the far side of the dining-room, alone, wearing a dark blue double-breasted suit and a scarlet necktie. With the sun flooding down on him, he looked shockingly handsome—and worried. When he saw her, he jumped to his feet. 'Did you get lost?' he said, helping her with her coat, guiding her into her seat.

'No, your directions were perfect. Am I late?'

'No, no, right on time.'

She could see that this was not going to be a casual, boozy get-together like their dinner at the Detroit Club. He was drinking coffee, and she ordered a cup, black.

When the waiter left, Ted took a good long look at the golf-course and then turned to her. 'You remember me asking you to think about the people you worked with on the '54s and whether or not they seemed loyal?'

'Yes.'

'Well?'

She paused until the waiter poured her coffee and withdrew.

'I can't imagine any of them doing what you talked about —giving away our work or selling it. It matters too much to everyone.'

'That's what I figured you'd say.' He sounded disappointed. 'That's why I asked you here today, Claire. Would you see if you can find a reason why anyone who worked on the '54s might sell us out? It could be just about anything—a debt, a grudge against the company, a bribe, a girl-friend, greed, anything. All I'm looking for is a motive.'

'Are you sure about this, Ted? I mean, you say the Plymouth's front bumper looks like ours, and maybe it does in a way. But the resemblance isn't all *that* close.'

'Let me explain something to you.' He lit a cigarette. 'We're the second largest division in the largest corporation in the world. When you're that big, you can't afford to take any chances. This business is built on the annual model change, and the annual model change is built on secrecy. It's the number one thing we sell. If your secrets start getting away from you, you're in deep shi– excuse me, you're in serious trouble. That's why I can't afford the luxury of sitting around and wondering. I've got to act, and I've got to act now. Do you understand so far?'

'Yes.'

'You don't have to get involved in this. I'm asking you as a personal favor.'

'What happens if I say no?'

He looked away. 'Nothing happens.'

She looked out the window. This was not what she'd expected.

'Tell me what you're thinking,' Ted said.

'I still find it hard to believe that someone would actually sell our designs.'

'Believe me, it's been going on for years. When you've got something valuable, there's always someone who'll try to get it. It's the oldest story in the book.'

'Suppose it's true and I find out who did it. What's in it for me?'

He looked down at his hands and smiled. 'I like that,' he said.

68

'What do you like?'
'I like a person who isn't afraid to look out for himself.'
'*Her*self.'
'Yes, herself.' He was still smiling. She imagined it was a smile of triumph. He squeezed her hand. 'Believe me, Claire, I've got big plans for you.'

16

On the two-hour flight to New York, Ted Mackey was so distracted he couldn't concentrate on the newspaper accounts of Joe DiMaggio and Marilyn Monroe's honeymoon. He looked across the aisle at Will Lomax, surrounded by note cards, chewing a pencil, polishing the speech that Ted would give that evening to the Greater New York Buick Dealers Association. By the end of the year, Ted intended to have delivered it dozens of times and wanted the speech to be just right—part pep talk and part declaration of war, a pat on the back and a stick of dynamite up the ass, announcing that the good old days of the seller's market were over and that power had shifted from the dealerships to the factory. From now on, Detroit was calling the shots. Ted Mackey wanted the world to know that he was Detroit.

He ordered another Scotch from the stewardess and turned back to Sidney Skolsky's story in *Photoplay*. After spending fifteen hours in the Clifton Motel in Paso Robles on their wedding night, the newly-weds had continued on into the mountains above Palm Springs, where they hid away in a friend's cabin. 'There weren't any other guests,' Marilyn told her favorite gossip columnist. 'Joe and I took long walks in the snow. There wasn't even a television set. We really got to know each other. And we played billiards. Joe taught me how to play.'

The very thought of Joe DiMaggio spending his honeymoon teaching Marilyn Monroe how to play billiards struck Ted all wrong. If DiMaggio had anything to teach Marilyn Monroe, it was that even the most ecstatic cheers can turn to boos in the wink of an eye. Perhaps no other man in the world was more intimately acquainted with the fragile nature of fame and power. In 1938, after two brilliant seasons with the Yankees, young DiMaggio had demanded a pay hike from $15,000 to $40,000, a whopping sum in a country still grinding through the Depression. The Yankees were owned by a rich and dapper beer baron, Colonel Jacob Ruppert, who, ruling the club with an iron fist, was repelled by the thought that his young star might send players' salaries through the roof. If DiMaggio got $40,000 in 1938, what would an established star like Lou Gehrig demand in 1939? The Colonel made a final offer of $25,000. DiMaggio stuck to his demand. Negotiations broke off, and the great hold-out began.

Like millions of Americans, Ted Mackey, then a twenty-seven-year-old regional sales manager covering the southeastern states for Buick, could not resist the sports pages that spring. Wherever he went—Detroit, Atlanta, New Orleans—he devoured every scrap of news about the hold-out. The newspapers had joined the battle, generally siding with the Colonel and helping tilt public opinion against DiMaggio. The tide turned against the Yankee Clipper.

Two days after the season opened, DiMaggio accepted the Colonel's offer. But when he returned to the vast pasture of center field in Yankee Stadium, the star, accustomed to adoring cheers, heard boos and catcalls. One day a tomato splattered on the back of his head. He took to smoking a whole pack of cigarettes before every game. Colonel Ruppert was delighted. Life would never again be so simple for Joe DiMaggio.

And now, DiMaggio was spending his honeymoon teaching Marilyn Monroe to play billiards.

At the Essex House the Buick dealers of New York gave Ted Mackey a hero's welcome. They loved him. His '50 for 50' campaign had made them rich, and they viewed him as one of their own, a salesman at heart, a marketing genius, someone in Detroit who spoke their language and returned their phone calls.

Ted's after-dinner speech opened with a characteristic zinger: 'It's not a cheaper car that people want—it's an expensive car that costs less. And that's just what we're giving them with the new '54 Century!'

But as soon as the crowd was warmed up, his tone changed. This was not a pep talk. 'The seller's market is a thing of the past, a wonderful little fantasy that died in the summer of '53. Nobody will be able to sell Buicks at full price. Nobody.' He paused. 'We're gunning for number three this year, and our production quotas are up ten per cent. That means you're going to have to move a hell of a lot more iron. Forget the big mark-up. The name of the game now is high volume. If you can't sell what we ship, then we'll put another unit a few miles down the road from you—because we *will* sell every car we make this year. And next year. And the year after that.'

By the end of the speech, the lobster and filet mignon were sitting uneasily in a few stomachs. Later, in the hospitality suite, after the wives had gone to bed and the whisky had begun to flow, the dealers' mood turned to panic. Ted worked the room, jacket off, tie loose, shirt-sleeves rolled up, drink in his fist, pure Detroit. He argued, cajoled, teased, flattered, bullied, threatened. He did to the dealers what they do to their customers. The air was stale and blue, and the die-hards had started pouring their own drinks, stirring them with their index fingers. They pleaded with Ted not to dump cars on them; he promised he wouldn't; they knew he was lying; he knew they knew. He watched, delighted, as they staggered out the door one by one, shaking their heads, muttering to themselves.

17

Claire Hathaway kept thinking of Ted Mackey's words that day at the Country Club of Detroit: 'When you've got this much to lose, you can't afford to take any chances.'

The spying started innocently enough. One night, when everyone was working late, Claire decided to open with grapeshot. 'Is it just me,' she called out, 'or is the front bumper on this year's Plymouth a spitting image of ours?'

'Hadn't noticed,' Rory Gallagher said.

'Me neither,' Emily Buhner said.

'Well, I noticed,' Amos Fuller said. 'When I seen them two bulbs, I figured their stylists must be a bunch a tit men, just like us.'

'Amos, you're disgusting,' Emily said. 'For your information I am not a tit man.'

'Y'ain't telling me something I don't know!'

'Come on, you guys, I'm serious,' Claire said. 'The Plymouth has a Dagmar bumper exactly like ours.' But no one took the bait, not even Norm Slenski, who was always first to weigh in with a pointless opinion on any subject. Even when she got her co-workers alone—at lunch, in the Tech Center corridors, at parties—she got nowhere. And she continued to get nowhere until the night Norm offered to take her on a guided tour of the gambling dens of Hamtramck.

Hamtramck was one of the most purely Polish neighborhoods west of Warsaw, a wide open, deliriously corrupt, blue-collar Catholic city within a city that had earned the nickname 'Wild West of the Middle West'. The tour began at ZZ's, across the railroad tracks from Dodge Main. Shortly after midnight, when the second shift finished, the place changed from a sleepy social club to a rollicking crapshoot. Claire couldn't believe her eyes. Assembly line workers in grimy overalls were betting their entire paychecks on dice rolls, with the winners scooping up armfuls of cash. The place filled with smoke and cursing and laughter and polka music. One loser wept on Norm Slenski's shoulder. 'My old lady's gonna murder me! Norm, buddy, spot me a fifty till Monday!'

From ZZ's they went to the Kosciusko Club, the Knights of Columbus and a joint with no name, just a single yellow light bulb burning over the front door. Everywhere they went, Norm kept winning. He played poker, darts, craps, rummy, punchboards; he even flipped a guy for fifty dollars, called heads—and won. By four o'clock he was warmed up, but Claire had seen enough. Any man who gambled like that could certainly wind up in need of some quick cash.

'Don't these joints ever close?' she said, when they stepped out on to the sidewalk and stood under the yellow light bulb.

'Why should they? They'll be packed again as soon as the graveyard shift gets off.'

She could see the jagged roof line of Dodge Main a few blocks away and hear the whirr and clang and hiss of the assembly line. 'So,' she said, 'that's where they make the fucking Plymouths, eh?'

'Whatta you got against Plymouth? If it wasn't for Dodge Main there wouldn't be no Hamtramck.'

'I'll tell you what I've got against Plymouth. They've been stealing our designs right out from under our noses.'

'Says who?'

'Says me. Says a lot of people. Come on, Norm, you've been around longer than anybody. You've seen the '54 Buick and you've seen the '54 Plymouth. Does their front bumper look like an accident to you?'

'Who cares?'

'I do. It makes me furious. I'd like to know who's selling us out.'

'What's it worth to you?' He was grinning. He leaned against the wall of the building and started twirling a strand of her hair between his fingers. In the yellow light his round face reminded her of a harvest moon in Iowa. He was such a moron—and yet he'd come up with the perfect question, the only question: What was it worth to her? She hadn't even asked herself.

18

Morey Caan gazed out the train window at the petrochemical badlands of New Jersey. He'd been unable to shake the feeling that this trip was unwise. Big news was breaking every day in Washington, such a steady staccato of sensational stories that he almost wished he was still working for a daily newspaper. Almost.

It had started with the hydrogen bomb mishap in the Pacific. Then Robert Oppenheimer was suspended by the Atomic Energy Commission and a 'blank wall' was placed between him and all classified information. Now the Army–McCarthy hearings were

underway, and Ike had just unveiled the 'domino theory', his fear
that, if the United States allowed the French to lose Vietnam to
the communists, then a whole string of calamities would
ensue—the fall of Laos, then Cambodia, Thailand, Burma,
Malaysia, Indonesia, eventually the Philippines, Formosa and
Japan, possibly Australia and New Zealand and finally, no
doubt, New Mexico and New Jersey.

Already he was missing last week's intoxicating roll-call,
beginning with the press conference that starred Ike and Lewis
Strauss of the Atomic Energy Commission. After a brief opening
statement, Ike turned the podium over to Strauss, a short, natty
bundle of energy who'd made his fortune advising the
Rockefellers how to manage theirs. Now he was the most vocal
proponent of the H-bomb and, therefore, a bitter enemy of J.
Robert Oppenheimer, the bomb's most vocal opponent.
There Strauss stood, balding, bespectacled, viciously precise,
surrounded by maps and charts as he explained to the press that
the 'Bravo' test had gone almost as planned.

'The wind failed to follow prediction that day and shifted
south,' he read from a prepared statement, 'and the little islands
of Rongelap, Rengerik and Utirik were in the path of the fall-
out. A Japanese fishing trawler, *The Fortunate Dragon*, appears
to have been missed in our search of the area. But based on a
statement from her skipper to the effect that he saw the flash of
the explosion and heard the concussion six seconds later, it must
have been well within the danger area.'

The Fortunate Dragon! Magnificent irony for the atomic age,
Morey thought as he scribbled in his notebook. Strauss went on
to say that all 236 natives of the three islands had been evacuated
and placed under medical supervision, that he had visited them
personally and found them 'happy and well.' One woman gave
birth to a healthy girl, which she named after Strauss's wife,
Alice. Since the natives have no use for money, Strauss gave the
woman ten pigs.

He asked if there were any questions.

After taking care of the big-hitters in the front row, Strauss
pointed at Morey. 'Admiral Strauss,' he said, rising to his feet,
'can you describe the area of the blast, the effectiveness of the

blast, and give us a general description of what actually happened when the H-bomb went off?'

'The area,' Strauss said, 'if I were to describe the area specifically, that would be translatable into the number of megatons involved, which is a matter of military secrecy. You said the effectiveness—I don't know what you mean by that.'

'Many people have been groping for some information as to what happens when an H-bomb goes off, how big the area of destruction is. I'm asking for some enlightenment on the subject.'

'Well, the nature of the H-bomb is that, in effect, it can be made to be as large as you wish, as large as the military requirements demand. That is, an H-bomb can be made large enough to take out a city.'

'A whole *city*?' Morey knew that every reporter in the room had cried out with him.

Strauss blinked. 'Yes, a whole city, destroy a city.'

'How big a city?' Morey said.

'Any city.'

'Any city. New York?'

'The metropolitan area, yes.'

'Washington, D.C.?'

'Oh, certainly.'

Morey was drowned out as a dozen reporters started shouting questions. It was, he thought now as the train entered the tunnel for the final approach to New York, the finest moment of his career. The Administration then spent a solid week clarifying Strauss's remark, trying to contain the hysteria about the power of this new generation of bombs.

The Oppenheimer press conference yesterday was a different kind of thrill. Morey showed up early and got a good seat in the third row.

Ike tried to make the investigation of Oppenheimer's security file sound routine. Everyone in the room knew better, and they all had the same question: If the man who oversaw the development of the atomic bomb isn't safe from the Red hunters, then who is?

Throughout the question-and-answer period, Morey kept waving his hand in the air. Finally, when Ike had taken care of all his pets and the heavyweights, he pointed at Morey. 'Yes, you there in the red necktie.'

'Mr President,' he said, 'will Dr Oppenheimer's past service to the country, particularly his contributions to the development of the atomic bomb, have a bearing on this investigation?'

Ike cleared his throat. 'I have known Dr Oppenheimer and, like others, I have certainly admired and respected his very great professional and technical attainments and this is something that is the kind of thing that must be gone through with what I believe is best not talked about too much until we know whatever answers there might be.'

Morey could feel the stunned silence around him. Pens had stopped scratching notebooks. He was powerless to resist. 'Mr President,' he said, 'would you mind repeating that?'

He sat down to roaring laughter. Ike, who never forgot a slight and rarely made the same mistake twice, surely made a mental note never to call on the frizzy-haired asshole again. But Morey didn't care. He had got the single best morsel yet for *Straight from the Horse's Mouth.*

19

Riding in from La Guardia in the black Buick limousine, Ted Mackey got started on the New York papers. They were loaded with accounts of Marilyn Monroe's reception in Japan.

DiMaggio had been invited there to conduct baseball clinics and smile for the cameras, an old and lucrative stick for the ex-Yankee. Marilyn had gone along, according to Louella Parsons, after promising to stay in the background and play the loyal wife while her husband took his turn in the limelight. But when the Pan Am Clipper stopped in Hawaii to refuel, there was a crowd at the airport for autographs and pictures—not of Joe. Reluctantly Marilyn obliged. In Tokyo the press dubbed her 'the honorable buttocks-swinging madam.' Mobs pawed her. A throng camped outside their hotel. Then an Army official invited her to sing for the troops still stationed in Korea.

Her performances in front of thousands of homesick, horny

soldiers were electrifying. Even after she agreed to tone down her act, reducing the writhing and cutting out the more suggestive songs, the troops continued to rampage. 'On two occasions,' the *New York Times* reported, 'troops rioted wildly and behaved like bobby-soxers in Times Square, not like soldiers proud of their uniforms.'

The coverage stopped abruptly when Marilyn returned to Tokyo, where she and Joe shut themselves in their hotel suite. What Ted Mackey didn't know, what even the most industrious gossip columnists were unable to dig up, was that an exchange took place in the privacy of their bedroom shortly after Marilyn's return from Korea. Still flushed from the adoring cheers and whistles and applause, Marilyn, dressed in a pink cashmere sweater and black toreador pants, rambled on about how wonderful it was to feel so desired, so loved. 'Joe,' she said dreamily, kicking off her shoes, sprawling on the bed, 'you've never *heard* such cheering.'

Joe DiMaggio had always been a man of few words.

Looking down at Marilyn Monroe stretched out on the bed, DiMaggio cleared his throat. He intended to speak. He believed he had many things to teach this woman, for he knew all about insomnia, ulcers and how cheers could turn overnight into catcalls and boos.

But DiMaggio did not say these things to his wife. He wouldn't have known how. Instead he fixed her with his heavy-lidded Sicilian stare and said, 'You think I never heard such cheering? You need to think again.'

Their marriage was over. She had the power to drive crowds wild. It was crazy not to use it.

That night Ted Mackey threw a dinner party in the back room of Toots Shor's for the top ten New York Buick dealers and the stylists he'd brought from Detroit for the opening of the year's first Motorama. Ted loved this restaurant because Toots called him Theodore and the clientele consisted of just enough showbiz types—sports figures, bookies, newspaper-men and ticket hustlers—for Ted to feel he was in touch with the real New York.

As the party was breaking up, Ted drew Claire Hathaway aside. 'There's something we need to talk about,' he said. 'In private. Take a cab and meet me at El Morocco. It's on East 54th Street. The cab driver'll know the place. I'll be waiting out front.'

'But I'm supposed to go to Greenwich Village with Amos and—'

'Tell them you've got a headache. I'll see you in fifteen minutes.'

Twelve minutes later, Claire walked into El Morocco. Out front limousines were double-parked; inside women were in white satin and glittery gowns, men in tuxedos. There were papier-mâché cactus plants and palm trees and zebra-striped banquettes. On the dance floor the couples looked like they were glued together.

The *maître d'* seemed to know Ted and led him and Claire to a small round table in the corner, under a canopy of palm fronds. A woman in pink pulled up a chair, hiked her skirt up over her knees and started pounding on a pair of bongos.

'This is some place,' Claire said.

'I figured it was about time you saw how the other half lives,' Ted said, fixing drinks from the bottle of Johnnie Walker that, along with the ice bucket and seltzer bottle, had been brought by the waiter without him having to be told. Ted handed her a drink and raised his glass. 'A toast to . . . to finally seeing you outside the city limits of Detroit, far from the prying eyes of the world.'

'I'll drink to that.'

'I've been trying to reach you at home all week,' Ted then said abruptly, 'but you're never in. Very bad form, don't you agree?' There was a trace of fatherly reprimand in his voice.

'I've been working a lot of late nights.'

'You could've called.'

'I guess the reason I haven't is because I haven't come up with much on anyone in the Beauty Parlor. About the only thing worth mentioning is that Norm Slenski gambles like a drunken Indian. I'm not much of a spy, I'm afraid.'

Ted's hand fell on hers, casually, almost as though by accident. But it stayed there. She looked at the blue veins snaking

through the soft black hairs, the gold wristwatch peeking from the starched white shirt cuff. It was such a strong hand, so warm. 'Don't apologize. That information about Slenski could come in very handy. As a matter of fact, he's our prime suspect.' She felt him squeeze her hand. She squeezed back. 'Enough shop talk,' he said. 'I've got some news for you.'

'Good news?'

'Excellent news. So excellent, in fact, that it requires champagne—which just happens to be on ice right now in my suite at the Plaza.'

She didn't say a word. She simply stood up and held out her arm.

20

On the day, six months later, that Buick set an all-time sales record, everyone involved with the design of the 1954 line was invited to a party at Ted Mackey's house. Everyone except Norm Slenski, of course.

Claire Hathaway, Amos Fuller and Rory Gallagher were out on the glassed-in porch inhaling cocktails. They had grown depressed talking about the decision to shelve the Wildcat and now stood about listening to Amos. He was talking about his boyhood hero, Berry Gordy, and the record company he was trying to start.

'He's calling it Motown—MO-tor TOWN, dig?—and he needs people like us. People to design record covers, posters, stage sets, even costumes for the acts. Think how hip it would be!'

'Um, Amos,' Rory said, 'I hate to rain on your parade, but we design cars for a living.'

'You mean we *used* to,' Amos said.

'He's got a point,' Claire said. 'They've had me working on a gear shift lever for the '57 Roadmaster.'

'And I'm doing instrument dials,' Rory said.

'And I been hiding out in the men's room,' Amos said.

Claire laughed but was then nearly overcome by a wave of

nausea. She excused herself and hurried down the hall toward the foyer. Just as she reached the bathroom, she heard Ted's wife callout behind her, 'Harvey, there you are! Come here, darling, I've got something to tell you.'

Claire stepped into the bathroom, leaving the light off and the door ajar. The clacking of Milmary's high heels stopped just a few feet from the bathroom door. Claire held her breath.

'I've got some wonderful news,' Milmary said. Claire leaned closer to the door. She fought off another wave of nausea and steadied herself against the wall. Milmary whispered, 'I'm pregnant!'

'That's . . . that's wonderful, dear,' Harvey said. 'Congratulations! But I thought you'd decided two was enough.'

'I changed my mind. Can you keep a little secret?'

'Of course.'

'Ted doesn't even know yet. You know how it happened?'

'Yes, my dear, I know all about the birds and the bees.'

'No, silly. I used a hat pin.'

'A hat pin?'

'I used it to poke a hole in Ted's condoms—right through the foil. He had no idea.'

'Why would you do a sneaky thing like that?'

'Because I made up my mind I wanted to have a baby and knew Ted would try to talk me out of it.'

Their footsteps receded down the marble tiles and disappeared into the buzz in the living-room. Claire heard Ted's booming laugh. She locked the door and turned on the light and in one smooth motion leaned over the black marble sink and vomited.

21

At ten o'clock in the morning on the last day of 1954, the General Motors board of directors met to clear up some routine year-end business. The atmosphere in the oak-panelled board room was upbeat, almost jovial.

There was good reason for the high spirits. Preliminary sales

figures indicated that Chevrolet had outsold Ford to remain the most popular car in America, and that Buick had edged Plymouth to finish number three. Nineteen fifty-four would surely be the most profitable year in the history of the corporation, with fat bonuses for executives and handsome dividends for stockholders. Despite the early hour, several board members lit cigars.

The board gave its undivided blessing to President Harlowe Kurtz's realignment of several top management positions. Ted Mackey, who had guided Buick to its best year ever, was being put in charge of the new Market Research Division. Though this was a lateral move at best, Mackey would receive a ten per cent salary increase. Walter Chrisman, Oldsmobile's general manager, would take over at Buick. There was no debate because the board members had already been briefed by Kurtz that the decision to go with such a brash young general manager as Mackey at Buick had been a mixed success. Mackey had outsold Plymouth, but he had also spent a lot of time and money trying to plug design leaks and pursuing a Hollywood actress, and had been forced to shelve a promising new car. Rumors were now circulating that one of his PR stunts was about to backfire and produce a damaging article in *Life* written by a frizzy-haired asshole from Washington, D.C. Clearly, the division needed a steadying influence at the helm.

Ted Mackey was not yet aware of any of this. He had no idea that his career had suddenly stalled, or that tomorrow his wife would announce that she was pregnant with their third child. As the board of directors' meeting droned on into the afternoon, Ted was at home giving orders to the caterers who were getting the big white house ready for his annual New Year's Eve bash. The guest list was longer and more prestigious than ever. Claire Hathaway wouldn't be coming, of course, but the party had already been written up in the *Detroit Free Press*.

Beyond that, all Ted Mackey knew for sure was that Buick had outsold Plymouth in 1954 and that he had the warmest feeling in the world, the feeling that after all the years of struggle and striving he had, at long last, arrived.

JEREMY RIFKIN
ANATOMY OF A
CHEESEBURGER

Jeremy Rifkin

R ay Kroc, one of the founders of the McDonald's hamburger chain, changed American eating habits as effectively as Henry Ford changed the way Americans travel. He understood the vast market created by highways and suburbs; the new form of transportation required a new kind of food—*fast*—and by the mid-1950s the hamburger had clearly become the premier fast food in the United States, eclipsing the previous national 'dish', the American apple pie. Today, 200 Americans purchase one (or more) hamburgers every second, and each American consumes twenty-seven-and-a-half pounds of ground beef every year.

Ray Kroc first sited his restaurants near churches, wanting to create a hamburger sanctuary: a place where pilgrims could rest and be refreshed, knowing that everything would be orderly and predictable, according to a secular catechism. Uniformity and speed were the important features: the process of making a hamburger was broken into its components, and each task was written out in precise detail. Nothing was to be left to personal initiative or guesswork. There was a 385-page operating manual, McDonald's bible, and deviation from it was never tolerated.

Kroc began by standardizing beef patties: each one was to weigh 1.6 ounces, measure 3.875 inches in diameter and contain no organs or grains. The bun was to be three and a half inches wide, high in sugar content so that it could brown quickly. There would be a quarter of an ounce of onion.

Kroc left nothing to chance. In his memoir he recalls the care paid to the choice of wax paper used to separate the hamburger patties:

> It had to have enough wax on it so that the patty would pop off without sticking when you slapped it on to the griddle. But it couldn't be too stiff or the patties would slide and refuse to stack up. There was also a science in stacking the patties. If you made the stack too high, the one on the bottom would be misshapen and dried out. So we arrived at the optimum stack, and that determined the height of our meat suppliers' packages.

Henry Ford said of his Model T, 'I don't care what colour

they want as long as it's black.' The same principle of uniformity could have applied to Kroc's hamburgers. Each one was the same, *always*, and customers were discouraged from garnishing theirs according to individual taste: to do so would slow up the line, and increase the expense of production. In his memoirs Kroc is adamant:

> The minute you get into customizing, you're on an individual basis. The cost of the product is exactly the same, but the labour triples. We can't do that.

Kroc allocated 'fifty seconds' to serve a McDonald's hamburger, shake and fries.

2

Although most economic historians have studied the steel and automobile industry in seeking an explanation for America's early industrial development, it was in the stockyards of Chicago that many innovations in industrial design were introduced. Meat-packing was the first American industry to use assembly lines.

In the older process, a steer would first be stunned, impaled and left to bleed on the ground, and three or four men would then drag the dead beast along the floor to a cross-tie, where it would be propped up to allow the head to swing free. The process could take fifteen minutes or more. By the first decade of the twentieth century, after the introduction of assembly line techniques, one 'shackler' could hoist seventy carcasses in a minute. Henry Ford acknowledged that his production ideas 'came in a general way from the overhead trolley that the Chicago packers used in dressing beef.'

The early industrial slaughterhouses were dimly lit and poorly ventilated and workers stood in pools of stagnant water, full of effluent and blood, eating their meals nearby, surrounded by sawed and sectioned limbs and carcasses. Accidents were common, especially on the killing floor where workers, brandishing knives and saws, would have to dress their own wounds themselves without slowing up operations on the line.

In 1904 Upton Sinclair wrote *The Jungle*, a devastating exposé of the beef-packing industry. The book shocked America with its graphic descriptions of unsanitary conditions in the slaughterhouses of Chicago.

> Whenever meat was so spoiled that it could not be used for anything else . . . they [the packers] either canned it or else chopped it into sausage . . . There was never the least attention paid to what was cut up for sausage; there would come all the way from Europe old sausage that had been rejected, and that was mouldy and white—it would be dosed with borax and glycerine, and dumped into the hoppers, and made over again for home consumption. There would be meat that had tumbled out on the floor, in the dirt and sawdust, where the workers had trampled and spit uncounted billions of consumption germs. There would be meat stored in great piles in rooms; and the water from leaky rooms would drip over it, and thousands of rats would race about on it. It was too dark in these storage places to see well, but a man could run his hand over these piles of meat and sweep off handfuls of dried dung of rats. These rats were nuisances, and the packers would put poison bread out for them; they would die, and then rats, bread and meat would go into the hopper together.

The angry public reaction forced Congress to pass the Pure Food and Drug Act of 1906, barring adulterated or mislabelled food from interstate commerce. That year Congress also passed a Meat Inspection Act, mandating federal inspection of all classes of livestock and of red meat in interstate and foreign commerce.

In recent years most Americans have come to believe that the meat they consume poses no serious health threats. The public's ease was shaken in the 1960s when Congressman Neal Smith of Iowa publicized health conditions in meat-processing plants not under any direct *federal* mandate. Many of the giant beef packers—Swift, Armour and Wilson—were by-passing federal inspection statutes by processing up to twenty-five percent of their red meat in so-called 'intra-state plants' and shipping the products only within the state, thus avoiding interstate commerce laws and federal inspection. Many states did not require that their livestock be inspected, and the conditions in packing facilities could be deplorable. According to a Department of Agriculture (USDA) report that was leaked to the press, inspectors had uncovered 'rodents and insects, in fact many vermin [which] had free access to stored meats and meat product ingredients.' In North Carolina they had seen 'snuff-spit [and] sausage meat fallen on the same floor which was then picked up and shoved into the stuffer.' In Norfolk, Virginia, federal authorities 'found abscessed beef and livers, abscessed pork livers, parasitic livers mixed with edible products.' In Congressional hearings, legislators were told of the widespread practice of buying what packers called '4D livestock'—dead, dying, diseased and disabled—to cut expenses.

Even today, unsanitary conditions remain widespread. In a 1985 report, the National Academy of Sciences found that federal inspection procedures were inadequate. The report recommended that 'newer technologies . . . and modified slaughtering and dressing techniques be developed and implemented to reduce infections and other hazardous agents.' The recommendations have not been acted on.

3

This is a short biography of a modern cow.

One of the most important things for a rancher to know about his herd is when cows are in heat, and in the United States this knowledge is gained in a number of ways. One is by using 'sidewinders' or 'teaser bulls'. The teaser bull has been fixed by a surgical operation that re-routes his penis so that it comes out of his side. When the bull becomes aroused in the presence of a cow in heat, he attempts to mount her, but is unable to penetrate the vagina; however, he does leave a coloured dye on her rump from a marker that has been hung around his chin, and ranchers are then able to identify the cows that need to be sequestered and artificially inseminated.

Drugs are used for the same purpose: one drug—produced by the Upjohn company and marketed for its efficiency (its advertising slogan is 'You call the shots')—is injected into all cows in a herd at once so that they come into heat at the same time. By synchronizing the oestrus cycles, ranchers can choose the ideal time for calving.

For a short period after birth, young heifers enjoy a sort of freedom. They are allowed to run with their mothers for six to eight months on the open range. Thereafter they are transported to mechanized feed lots—there are around 42,000 in the United States, although most cattle end up at one of the 200 largest ones. A feed lot is a fenced-in area with a concrete feed trough on one side of it, where thousands of cattle are fed together at one time.

Before being fattened, calves are dehorned to ensure that they do not injure one another. Although a chemical paste is used that burns the horns to the roots, some ranchers use an electronic dehorner that cauterizes the horn tissue. Others simply use saws. After dehorning, there is the next stage: castration. A castrated bull is 'docile' and yields beef of better quality. The scrotum is stretched and punctured by a knife so that the sac can be cut open: it is then possible to pull out the testicles and cords.

The next stage involves growth-stimulating hormones. Anabolic steroids, in the form of time-release pellets that are implanted in the animals' ears, improve weight gain by five to twenty per cent and feeding efficiency by five to twelve per cent. Over ninety-five per cent of feed-lot-cattle in the United States receive hormones, even though many of these are suspected of triggering a wide range of cancers in humans. Diseases, prevalent in the cramped pens and feed lots, are fought by massive doses of antibiotics: in 1988 over fifteen million pounds of antibiotics were used as feed additives for livestock. According to a report issued by the National Academy of Sciences, sixty per cent of all cattle and other livestock will have been fed antibiotics at some point in their lives (and will account for over half the antibiotics manufactured in the United States). It is common for antibiotic residues to appear in the meat sold in supermarkets.

The cattle feed itself is worth examining. It is saturated with herbicides and insecticides; in fact it has been contaminated long before it reaches the feed trough. Eighty per cent of herbicides and insecticides used in the United States are sprayed on corn and soybeans—they are the main feed for cattle and other livestock—and are then retained in the fatty tissue of the animal over its lifetime. The feed is not simply 'feed': to reduce costs, it is regularly mixed with cardboard, newspaper and sawdust. Manure from chicken houses and pig pens is also added. Cement dust has recently become an attractive supplement, according to the United States Department of Agriculture, because it 'produces weight gains thirty per cent faster.'

After being fattened to their 'ideal' weight of 1,000 pounds, mature steers are herded into trailers for the journey to the slaughterhouse—a journey that may involve travelling along the Interstate highways for several days, during which time it is impossible to stop for rest or nourishment—sometimes not even for water. On the way animals fall and are trampled, breaking legs and pelvises. The injured animals are called 'downers'. On arriving, the animals are led to a holding pen; downers—lying spread-eagled on the floor, unable to stand, or chained together by their broken legs—must wait to be unloaded. The animals who have died en route also have a name. They are called the 'dead pile'.

The steer, on entering the slaughterhouse, is stunned by a pneumatic gun, and, as it sinks to its knees, a worker hooks a chain on to a rear hoof, and hoists and then hangs it upside-down. The steer's throat is slit; a quick thrust of a worker's blade deep into the larynx severs the jugular vein and carotid artery. The blood is considerable. One writer describes the scene in this fashion:

> The kill floor looks like a red sea . . . warm blood bubbles and coagulates in an ankle deep pool. The smell sears the nostrils. Men stand in gore . . . each night the gooey mess is wiped away.

The dead animal, moving along the main 'disassembly line', is skinned (the hide is cut open at the stomach and stripped off in one piece by a machine), the carcass decapitated, the tongue split and removed, and both head and tongue impaled on hooks. The carcass is then gutted—liver, heart, intestines are removed—and cut down the centre of the backbone with power saws. The tail is pulled off. The split carcass is hosed down with warm water, wrapped in cloth and put in a meat cooler for twenty-four hours. This is where the meat is 'aged'. At meat plants, workers use the power saw the next day to divide the carcass into our familiar cuts of beef, which are tossed on to conveyor belts manned by thirty to forty boners and trimmers who prepare and box the final products. The neatly shaped cuts of beef, now vacuum-packed, are ready to be shipped to supermarkets across America.

There are 100 million cows in the United States, nearly one for every two-and-one-half Americans. Livestock, mostly cattle, consume almost twice as much grain as the entire population of the country.

4

In modern cattle production a 1,000 pound steer 'dresses out' to approximately 620 pounds of carcass after being disassembled on the slaughterhouse floor. The carcass yields about 540 pounds of retail meat products. Cuts of beef include round steak, top round, bottom round, rolled rump, rump roast, sirloin steak, porterhouse steak, T-bone steak, club steak, flank steak, rolled flank, hind flank, standing rib roast, rib steak, pot roast, ground beef, beef brisket, corned beef and short ribs.

In fact, only sixty per cent of the slaughtered steer is directed to human and pet consumption. The remaining forty per cent—fat, bones, viscera, hide—is converted by renderers into materials used in the production of other goods. Collagen, an element of connective tissue, is used in the preparation of glue. Collagen-based adhesives are used in wallpaper, glues, bandages, emery boards and sheet rock. Gelatin is used in ice cream, candies, yoghurt and mayonnaise, as well as in photographic

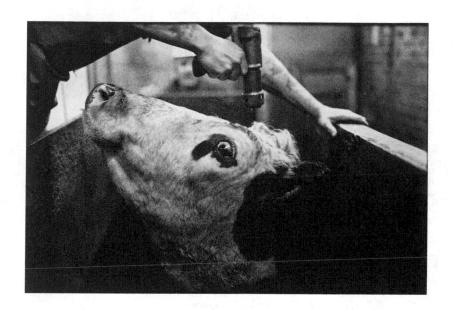

film and phonograph records. Beef fat and fatty acids are used in shoe cream, crayons, floor wax, oleo margarine, cosmetics, deodorants, detergents, soaps, perfumes, insecticides, linoleum, insulation and freon. Hooves and horns are used in combs, piano keys and imitation ivory. Hides are used in leather goods, upholstery, shoes and luggage. Hair is used in paint brushes. Insulin from the pancreas is used to treat diabetes; glucagon from the pancreas to treat hypoglycaemia; tripsin and chymotrypsin to treat burns and wounds; pancreatin to aid digestion; cattle blood plasma to treat haemophilia and anaemia; thrombin as a blood coagulant; the intestines as medical sutures; bone marrow to treat people with blood disorders and to be used as the soft cartilage in plastic surgery; ACTH from the pituitary gland to alleviate arthritis and allergies. Cattle by-products are also used as binders for asphalt paving, as cutting oils and as industrial lubricants. In the beef industry they use everything but the 'moo'.

5

This is how the modern cow is inspected.

In the plants now inspected by the new 'speeded' system, federal meat authorities no longer examine every carcass on the production line. Instead, company employees conduct checks randomly—looking at as few as three heads out of 1,000. The employees, concerned about keeping their jobs, are not encouraged to stop contaminated beef; they are hardly unbiased judges. In one pilot programme, the company's quality-control staff failed to spot all tonsils infected with measles (they didn't know what tonsils were).

In their new, reduced capacity, federal inspectors look at fewer than one per cent of carcasses; they had formerly examined every animal that came down the line. They no longer check carcasses for disease. Kidneys, lymph nodes, tongues, lungs and heads are not inspected separately, unless a worker first indicates a problem. Federal inspectors no longer check equipment for microbic contamination. They are not even allowed to look at all sides of the carcass or touch the parts necessary to check for signs of disease (under the tongue, the glands). One inspector noted that 'because we no longer palpate or feel the tongues, cactus thorns and associated abscesses are getting through. We miss the flukes, abscesses, lungs and measles, because we can't palpate the diaphragm.'

Rinses are being used to mask contaminated carcasses. Under new procedures, cattle with fevers are hosed down until they cool off to an acceptable temperature, then killed.

In 1990, twenty-four Department of Agriculture inspectors sent a letter to the National Academy of Sciences raising questions on the wholesomeness of American beef. Standards have been so compromised, says one inspector, that 'meat whose disease symptoms previously would have forced it to be condemned, or, at most, approved for dog food, now gets the USDA seal of approval for consumers.' Inspectors cite the case of 'water bellies', cows that are clogged up with urine. 'There is the equivalent of buckets of urine in their briskets, shank and bellies. It just floods out when the cow is slaughtered.' Under the new inspection system, cow bellies are routinely approved for human consumption.

Cattle with peritonitis, a bloody mucous-like fluid in the carcass cavity, are approved; under the previous system they would have been condemned. Cattle with pneumonia and arthritis are also approved, as are those 'that wheeze loudly as they're breathing before slaughter and whose lungs are filled with fluid, that have scar tissue and abscesses running all up and down the sides of the lungs, and stuck to their ribs, and have popped blood vessels in kidneys that are no longer functional.' Cattle have been approved 'stuffed with regurgitated food that was oozing out.' Faecal smears up to a foot long, with hair, adhesions and flukes, are passing through. One Department of Agriculture inspector remembered seeing 'contamination due to faeces and hair from four feet away, mostly on the brisket, armpits and foreshanks.' Carcasses are sent down the line with their insides full of rust flakes, broken teeth, nails, claws, rings, tags, rosin. Conveyer belts become clogged with grease and cease functioning. Instead of cleaning the grease away, workers sprinkle salt on the machinery until the system can move again. In one plant, management refused to stop the line even 'when they were dripping hydraulic oil onto products' and then failed to tag the carcasses that were contaminated.

In some plants the walls in the rendering rooms are caked with scum and mildew. Two-inch-long cockroaches roam the floors. Meat being processed is so old it is green. This meat may already have been sent back from supermarkets because it was unwholesome: it is recycled. The gore and filth on the kill floors has attracted large numbers of rats. Rats are 'running on top of meat and gnawing at it.'

Contaminated heads, called 'puke heads' because they are filled with rumen content, are now being salvaged and reworked and no longer have to be submitted to the Department of Agriculture for re-inspection. In some plants a quarter of the puke heads that are being converted are contaminated with hair, dirt and ingesta. One inspector observed, 'Tonight some family is preparing to chow down on hamburgers, chili, etc, that contain ground-up trimmings from a head or heads like this.'

Meat processors and wholesalers are protesting over the increase in substandard meat being shipped from the packing plants. One sausage manufacturer became so distraught over the quality of beef being sent to him from some of America's major meat packers—including Monfort, Iowa Beef and Excel—that in 1989 he aired his grievances on television. He told of meat shipped to his plant that

> was obviously sour and full of bacteria. It stank and had pus from abscesses. Routinely the meat stinks so bad that government inspectors tell us to air it out.

RYSZARD
KAPUŚCIŃSKI
THE SOCCER WAR

'If you've wondered how Kapuściński managed to clock up twenty-seven revolutions...this book tells all, delivering in sentences short and lapidary a reality that suddenly flowers in images as rich and strange as anything in *Márquez*' - **Guardian**

'Part-diary, part-documentary account of the twenty years in which Kapuściński made the telex machines chatter with his unique reportage, his datelines forming a gazeteer of the world's trouble spots' - **Sunday Telegraph**

£5.99

GRANTA BOOKS

IVAN KLÍMA
THE NIGHT OF THE
RAILWAYMEN'S BALL

The season of ballroom dancing was upon us and crime was on the increase. I have little interest in ballroom dancing—I don't dance. A paedophile was at large in our neighbourhood and the school had warned us to keep our children off the streets. My daughter told me that coming back from aerobics with a younger friend, they had seen a stranger by the telephone booth on the corner who asked if they could give him two fifty-heller coins for a crown.

'So what did you do?'

'I only had one,' my daughter told me, 'but he gave me the whole crown for it anyway.'

The man asked them where they lived and where the Novaks lived. As fate would have it, the only Novak in our neighbourhood, Engineer Novak, happened to be walking by and when he introduced himself, the stranger took off. My daughter described him, but her description meant nothing to me.

Not long ago my wife's colleague, who works in a psychiatric institute, invited her to a club meeting for paedophiles. I went along. I was astonished to discover that most of the rehabilitated paedophiles looked not only utterly normal, but even rather sympathetic; they seemed gentle and restrained. Of course when they behave properly, my wife's colleague informed us, they are allowed to go home for the weekend.

'And they don't do anything wrong?' I asked.

'We tranquillize them before they leave,' she said, to allay my fears. 'But sometimes something goes wrong inside their heads and they don't come back on Monday. In such cases, the institute calls the police at once to avoid possible trouble. But the police have other things on their minds besides chasing after patients from the psychiatric institute, and so paedophiles, along with other escapees and as yet unexposed criminals, have the run of the city. As long as they don't actually assault anyone, no one but anxious parents gives them much thought.'

Since the conversation had turned to the organs of public security, the doctor reminisced about a schizophrenic wrestler who had once been a patient of hers. This wrestler had a theory

Photo: Bill Brandt

about life, or rather about death, that interested me the moment I heard it. He thought that death was engaged in an unending struggle for control of the world, and to that end, She hired various assistants. Death and Her assistants moved among us, the living, in constantly changing disguises. On green days, which the wrestler alone was able to determine, they would dress up in police uniforms. That was when they were most dangerous.

The wrestler would never harm a soul, the doctor went on, but on the green days he had to be kept away from policemen in uniform. If he saw one, he would attack. He was a powerful man anyway, but when the fit came upon him his strength was amplified. Not only would he take the officer's pistol and night stick away from him, he would remove his cap, rip off his epaulettes and try to strip him of his uniform. Then he'd throw everything down the sewer or stuff it into a garbage can and run. Most of the time the police caught him, took their private revenge, and then returned him to the institute with a warning.

I asked, not without a certain malicious satisfaction, how often he indulged in such delights. The doctor grew sad. They had scarcely let him out once every six months, and then only when they felt he had become completely quiescent. Last fall, however, he hadn't returned, and they found him a week later with a broken back in a field some distance from the institute.

So in fact, he hadn't been wrong.

The doctor shrugged her shoulders.

The borderline between the madman and someone with brilliant insight into things that remain a mystery to others, is usually infinitesimally narrow.

My daughter is afraid neither of perverts nor of those who should be trying to catch them. She seldom thinks about death, but when she sees through its disguises and glimpses it, she cries. As befits her fourteen years, however, she prefers to giggle even when there is no reason to. She loves driving fast, she's a secret smoker, and whenever she can find the excuse, she hangs out in the evening with fellow students of dubious reputation. When we take her to the theatre, she responds to the performance as though it were real life. Unlike me, she plays the piano, strums the guitar and the mandolin, and knows how to dance. She says that if I were willing, she'd teach me too.

My supply of willingness, however, has been exhausted in other areas.

'So how about it? Are you coming to the ball with us?'

I was trapped. So far, I had managed to avoid going to balls, but now my friends were trying to persuade me to overcome, just this once, what they called my negative relationship to dancing. I could hardly refuse them. My friends were among those hounded and harassed by the police, in some cases even more than me. My attendance at this particular ball, though the thought annoyed me, had ceased to be a simple matter of my relationship to dancing.

Almost all of my friends had signed Charter 77, which meant that they had committed themselves (in the words of the Charter) both *individually and as a community to work towards recognition and respect for civic and human rights in our country and in the world.* The authorities were firmly convinced that they and they alone were competent and entitled to protect the people and their rights, and they took the Charter as a declaration of war. The Charter signatories were picked up and interrogated; their flats were searched. When those carrying out orders discovered nothing more incriminating than ideas and books that they alone found offensive, the authorities had the Chartists thrown out of their jobs, put under surveillance, publicly vilified. Their passports and drivers' licences were confiscated, their telephones disconnected. This battle had gone on for a year, one side obstinately demonstrating the justice of their claims, the other side demonstrating their vast superiority in strength. One of my persecuted friends decided that the season of balls would be a good time to have some fun and relax.

The ball they were to attend was organized by the railway workers. Though my friends could not hold a ball on their own, they believed no one could object to their attending a function organized by a group as politically correct as the railway workers.

I suspected that the plan to join the railwaymen for an

evening could not remain a secret. I believed my friends were foolish to think that those in disguise would not begrudge them an evening of dancing. My wife and daughter, on the other hand, had begun discussing what they would wear the moment our friends offered us tickets.

The day of the ball was overcast. A chilly wind spread a sheet of smoke, soot and ash over the city, and the streets were covered with a slick film of dirt. Anticipating disaster, I drove with extra care and parked the car as far as possible from the hall where the dance was to take place. My wife had had her high-school graduation dress repaired and altered for the occasion, and she still looked like a young girl. My daughter had made herself a gown of shiny scarlet taffeta. It was her first real evening dress; I could see that she was rehearsing in her mind the moment when she would take off her coat and enter the ballroom.

The women concentrated on negotiating the damp, treacherous sidewalk while I looked around. I noticed that on Peace Square, where we were headed, white and yellow squad cars bearing the two large, widely ridiculed letters indicating the Public Security forces—VB—were parked in places where it was forbidden to stop. Another white and yellow car, its siren wailing, wheeled into the square and sped up to the hall.

Even I could see that the green day had arrived.

Usually at this time of year, the small park in front of the St Ludmilla Church is empty, but now it was filled with men who, judging from their appearance, were obviously not regulars in the park. Corruption was in the air, and if you listened closely you could hear a quiet scraping sound, like carborundum sliding over a scythe blade or at least over hidden stilettoes. Soon we ran into the first group of friends, who announced that we would not get into the ball. When the people at the door realized we were not railway workers, they would give us our money back and turn us away.

As far as I was concerned, it made no sense to go any further, but my wife and daughter protested. They had finally managed to drag me out to a dance, so we should at least see for ourselves if it was impossible to get in.

My wife took me by one arm, my daughter by the other, and they would almost have persuaded me to pretend to be a railwayman (which, by the way, as a child I had always longed to be) had my friend Pavel not suddenly appeared in the park, supported by his wife.

My friend Pavel is one of those people who are plagued by the notion that they must tell others how to live in order to make the world a better place. That's why he's constantly getting mixed up in politics. He may well have been slightly more involved than others; that would explain why he was the only one who had suffered a blow to the head when, earlier, the mass expulsion of would-be ballroom dancers had taken place.

His driver's licence had long been confiscated, so he was looking for someone to take him to see a doctor.

I had always wanted to be an engine driver. When I was a child, there was nothing exceptional about this: there were almost no cars then, and truck drivers had not yet become an object of childhood dreams. I can no longer say exactly what it was about being an engine driver that attracted me: whether it was the desire to control the motion of an enormous hunk of metal, or the lure of far-away places. Whatever it was, I could stand by the kitchen window for ages, staring down towards the tracks and waiting for a train to appear. Then, when I heard the puffing of the enormous machine in the distance and saw the approaching plume of smoke—and when it was dark outside the smoke was full of swirling sparks as tiny as stars in the sky that glowed and then died—I was gripped by a blissful sense of expectation, as though I were supposed to leave on that train, or as though I were expecting a visitor to arrive on it, perhaps from the heavens themselves, from where the train always seemed to emerge. At the time I did not know of those other freight trains that, on narrow, normal and wide-gauge tracks carried, and would continue to carry throughout most of my life, uncountable numbers of people whom She and her beaters and followers had singled out as victims.

The moment Pavel stepped into the car, he started telling us what had just happened to him, things that to him seemed incomprehensible. Then he stopped. It occurred to him that perhaps it might be better to remain silent about it all in front of my daughter. My daughter, in rather rough terms, reassured him that on the contrary, she found such experiences entertaining; at least they made up, in part, for the ruined evening. She unbuttoned her coat to reveal her ball gown.

I would like to have told my friend something of my wartime experiences, because they had helped me to understand many of the events that came later. I would like to have told him that I had learned how the persecution of a select sample of victims gave Her several advantages. Not only did it arouse fear among other innocent people, but it also gave those who were not included in the sample a sense of satisfaction that they were considered worthy of trust. I would like to have mentioned how this even encouraged the most anxious of citizens to lend a hand, at least in the most inconspicuous of ways, to Her efforts so that with the passage of time, remaining silent about Her work became second nature, an understandable and forgivable vice. I could have gone on to suggest that persecution of the innocent also satisfied a degenerate passion that circulates in the blood of many of Her assistants. However, the white and yellow car I could see behind us distracted me.

In the time that came before my wartime experiences, the famous Helada company made soap. Into the long boxes containing their soap, they put pictures of steam and diesel locomotives. They issued an album with spaces into which you were supposed to stick the pictures. I owned the album and gradually filled the spaces in it. When I leafed through the book before going to sleep and saw locomotives in colours I'd never seen them in, locomotives with magnificent red wheels or with blue or green flanks, I was overwhelmed with enthusiasm, and I imagined that I was the one who was allowed to move the rods and levers that controlled them.

I drove Pavel and his wife to the nearest health clinic. The yellow and white striped car that had followed us all the way like a faithful hyena parked by the curb behind me. Now that I was no longer distracted by driving, I could observe its crew. There were four of them. The man sitting next to the driver was saying something into his walkie-talkie. When he finished talking, he and the rest of them were obviously waiting for an answer. I imagined I could hear a hollow, loud-speaker voice coming from inside their car. Then one of the men got out, walked around my car and rapped on my window.

I opened it, and he asked to see my documents. My driver's licence was almost new, and the vehicle registration was in order, as was the car. He produced a breathalyser, and I blew into the tube, certain that not the tiniest drop of alcohol was circulating in my blood. He noted my innocence, even thanked me and said goodnight before returning to his car, from where he must have reported the results of his investigation by radio.

My collection was almost complete; I was only missing two cards, both of express-train locomotives. One was called *The Mikado*, the other was nicknamed *Passepartout*. Their stats were printed in my album, but I had no idea what noble shapes and outlines distinguished them from the rest. What good is an incomplete collection? Whenever I opened the album, I saw only those two empty spaces crying out to be filled. We had enough soap at home to last for at least three years. I couldn't get the missing pictures by trading for them at school, so I had already given up hope when our grocer invited me behind the counter and allowed me to open the soap boxes until I found the two missing engines.

The unusual pleasure of being behind a counter was even greater than the joy of at last finding the pictures I needed. I sensed, although I had no way of appreciating my discovery yet, that the man behind the counter, no matter how deeply he might bow to his customers, possessed the power to satisfy people's needs and desires. And anyone who has such power is like a king.

My first encounter with a real engine driver happened not long ago. He brought me a message from a friend of mine who lived outside Prague. The message vouched for its bearer, Martin B., and asked me to lend him something good to read.

Martin B. was not the kind of man I had imagined in my childhood commanding an enormous engine. He seemed too slight, too young, and moreover he was dressed in denim.

We talked about folk singers. He was proud of his tape collection of protest songs by singers who were mostly silenced, and of his collection of books by banned authors. He or his friends copied out these books by themselves. I expressed surprise that someone so young would devote his time to copying out books by unknown authors.

'You have to do something!' This was the hope that encouraged him and told him his actions had meaning. I nodded and asked him how he liked his work.

My question surprised him. He had never wanted to be an engine driver.

I said that as a boy, I had, very much. What had he wanted to be, then?

He laughed. The only thing he could remember was wanting to go hunting in Alaska. At school, he had directed a play about Jack London. London could not have imagined how anyone could enjoy doing the same thing all his life. They should allow everyone to do one job for a while, and then to do something completely different, or nothing at all. He said he would happily spend half a year on a number sixteen train if he could spend the same amount of time wandering about the world.

Would he go to Alaska?

He'd go to Denmark first.

Why Denmark?

Because they have a decent government there, he explained. And you can travel through the whole country by bicycle. After a long fast, you have to begin with small mouthfuls. Besides, Hamlet was prince of the Danes.

I could find no fault with his reasons.

He left with a parcel of extremely hard-to-get books. He said that if I really wanted, he would, as a favour, let me ride with him in the engine and allow me to drive it. Of course it would only be a freight train; someone like him could never get a better position; he was not sufficiently committed politically.

I didn't take his offer seriously, but that night I had a dream. I was walking through a desert landscape on a path between a railway line and a high wall. Suddenly, a gate opened in the wall ahead of me and a hissing steam engine emerged. It cut across my path and stopped in front of me.

I realized that this was the train I'd been waiting for and that I should quickly climb aboard one of its cars. Instead, I stared at the locomotive in fascination. It was a steely blue and it seemed to be very light, as if hollow. The front of it looked like any steam locomotive; smoke was even coming out of the smokestack. But the whole rear section looked like the exposed inside of a large clock. Cog-wheels, large and small, gleamed as though cast from pure gold. Through the small window I saw the engine driver's face, and his hands moving nimbly among the rods and levers. I wanted to call out to him, to ask him to let me climb aboard, but before I could bring myself to do it, the train started up and in an instant disappeared in the distance, leaving me alone by the track.

When I told my dream to my non-existent psychoanalyst, he persuaded me that the dream had nothing to do with how I had longed to drive a locomotive. I had merely seen an image of my desperation to overcome the isolation in which I have found myself for some time now. The train, especially this complicated steam engine, represented an unattainable community—shiny and attractive, even though unacceptably outmoded. It symbolized friendship, a sense of belonging, love. I wanted to climb aboard, but the train started up and disappeared, leaving behind the rail of hope as a reminder of missed opportunities.

When did I miss my chance? I can't answer that. People miss opportunities every day. One can only try not to miss them through laziness or fear.

Pavel returned with a bandage around his head. There was an unexpected satisfaction in his expression. The doctor, Pavel claimed, had let it be known he sympathized. Pavel forgot about his pain as soon as he thought others shared it with him.

My wife leaned over to me and whispered an offer to drive if I was too upset.

Why should I have been more upset than her?

She imagines, like most people, that anyone who spends some time in prison or in concentration camps will spend the rest of his days, at least subconsciously, in fear of losing his freedom.

In fact it is usually the other way around. Often it is those who know about prison only from hearsay who fear it most. Fantasy can be more frightening than reality. Or perhaps it is even simpler: those who have made it through once hope they will be able to make it through again; the rest don't know. They have nothing to base their hope on.

My experience of life so far led me to two simple, if contradictory, conclusions. The first one was: everything evil a person can imagine can in fact happen. The second derived from the first: nothing that will happen to me in life can be worse than what has already happened to me.

The yellow and white car continued to follow us, keeping as close as safety allowed. Perhaps they were afraid we would try to escape, or they wished to frighten me to the point where I would try to lose them. They'd be happy enough to stop me for speeding.

Yet why should we, who had done nothing wrong, try to escape?

I wondered how many such chases and harassments were taking place at that moment? I've heard it said that a crime is committed somewhere on earth every second. Yet there are no generally acceptable definitions of crime. In some places, crimes are kept a secret. Elsewhere it is a crime when a man goes to a railwaymen's ball with his wife and daughter. And who keeps count of crimes committed by criminals cleverly disguised as crimefighters?

But it is certain that at any moment, somewhere in the

world, there are those who are on the run from robberies, from raped women, from murders and from molested and abused children. The harassment we suffered is worth paying attention to for one reason alone: it was probably the most nonsensical, and therefore the most wasteful crime of all.

Europe is asking, Pavel had written in one of his recent feuilletons, which the young engine driver and others like him were probably copying out, *where is the liberty, equality and fraternity for which people bled under the Bastille? It is asking, how is all power to the Soviets working, for which people died beneath the Winter Palace? It is asking, when will this game of power end that is keeping us artificially divided, so that we cannot have today what the prophets of happier tomorrows promise in the future?*

Pavel asked this question in the name of Europe. But it was Pavel who received a blow to the head. It seems to me that if they beat someone for asking a question, it should at least be his most personal question—especially if he is a writer. If a writer asks in the name of Europe or his country, or the people, in whose name should the politicians ask? But then what should a writer do, when the politicians have long ago stopped asking questions and take care only that they may rule without interruption, regardless of how harmful their rule may be?

I drove Pavel and his wife across the entire city to their home, where they intended to sleep. When we parted, it occurred to me that I should get out with them and put my wife and daughter on a tram, or try to find them a taxi. But I assumed that the men in the yellow and white car were more interested in my fractious friend, and that as soon as he got out, they would disappear. So I now looked hopefully into the rear-view mirror.

They were following me. I turned into a narrow side-street. So did they. It seemed I had committed one of the crimes they do not like to leave unpunished: I had expressed my solidarity.

We could have stopped and got out of the car. But one feels a little more protected in a car. Many people think of the car as their second home and some prefer it to their real home, which offers them no change, no mystery, not even the excitement of speeding. It depends on the people—and on the car.

I continued on my way home. When I next looked into the rear-view mirror, I saw that my following had increased by another yellow and white car.

Mr Novak, the civil engineer, lived only a few buildings away from us, but until recently we had never actually talked. He was a good-looking person, and so was his wife. They had three children. They played golf together—at least I would occasionally see them loading golf-clubs into their Skoda. I think he saw his wife as a princess, and if he had been a prince he would certainly have wanted to provide her with more than golf; but he was just a civil engineer. Last New Year's Eve, we walked back from the bus-stop together. He'd had a little bit to drink and he was carrying a basket piled high with eggs. He spoke first. He said that they had recently lent him for a day one of my books that was circulating in manuscript, and that since then he'd been waiting for a chance to express his sympathy. He could well imagine what a difficult time I must be going through when I couldn't make a living at work I knew how to do.

Then he spoke about his own difficult times, and how often he had to demean himself before dull people he had no respect for, and how he suffered this humiliation only so that he would not lose his pay cheque, which was miserable enough anyway. Was it possible, he asked me, as though I were some clairvoyant, for life to go on in this hopeless direction? What, then, was a person here for and why should he remain? I wasn't certain if he meant his sojourn in our country, or on this earth.

He slipped a couple of eggs in my pocket, we wished each other a happy new year, and parted.

Several days later I saw him on a bitterly cold morning attending to a shiny Mercedes. He couldn't contain himself and asked me what I thought of it. Seven years old, but in wonderful condition. He and his wife had always longed for such a car and then an unrepeatable offer to buy this one came up; but he'd had to go into debt so deeply that if anything happened to him in the foreseeable future, his family wouldn't even be able to afford a wreath. And then, with a rag that he'd dipped in some foul-looking chemical substance, he polished the chrome.

We had already passed through the middle of town and through the Vysehrad Tunnel, beyond which was a straight stretch of road running alongside the Vltava river. We were scarcely five minutes from home. It was at this point that the second yellow and white car suddenly accelerated past the first car and past us. For a moment I dared to hope they were leaving us to do something more useful, but then a uniformed arm emerged from the window waving, according to regulations, the lollipop stick that meant stop. I braked, and so did the car behind us.

Two uniformed officers crawled out of the first car and walked towards me. I opened the door.

'Please get out, driver,' said one. 'Your documents.' He spoke to me in the tone he probably used with criminals he was arresting. He was the smaller and rounder of the two. The other one, who was more robustly built, remained a few steps behind him.

I objected that his colleague in the other car, which was still behind us, had already seen my documents. He wasn't interested. He held his hand out to me and waited until I handed the papers over. He leafed through them for a while, and then he said something that surprised me. 'Sir, the way you've been driving suggests to me you've been drinking. Are you willing to submit to a breathalyser test?'

I protested. After all, I had been tested an hour ago, and since then they'd been continually on my tail. It was highly unlikely that I would have drunk something while I was driving.

'Do you refuse to undergo the test?'

I sensed a trap, and besides, they were behaving like clowns, not me. I took the test.

He took the tube from me, turned his back, and declared that the tube had turned green. Was I aware of the consequences that this could have for me?

Though I had become used to most things, I was astonished. For years I had tried to stay out of the game that in this country is a substitute for politics, a game which one side plays dishonourably and sinfully, and the other side, though it plays honourably, plays in despair. I don't take sides. Not out of cowardice or calculation; it's just that I have neither the strength, nor the time, nor the capacity for the game.

I know that miserable political conditions influence everyone's life, mine included, but I would not dare to claim, not even to myself, that I am sure enough of what conditions are good to be able to persuade others.

I am not convinced that one has a right to one's own automobile, airplane, or the satisfaction of all one's needs at a time when most of mankind is hungry. I don't know whose side I should take in the struggles and wars I hear about and read about every day, even though I suspect that most of those struggles will quickly be forgotten, whereas the stories of Antigone or Hamlet will live as long as humanity itself.

But all my doubts have not stifled within me the awareness that injustice must be resisted.

The tube couldn't have turned green. Show it to me!

He replied that he was not required to show me the tube. So he was, after all, ashamed to confront his claim with reality. He then began, somewhat incoherently, to explain that there were cases of mild intoxication in which the liquid in the tube changed colour only slightly. It made no sense to show the tube to me because to my untrained eye, the colouration would be imperceptible. He was not suggesting that I had drunk a lot, but the tone of the liquid had altered and that meant I had failed in my duty as a driver and become a hazard on the road. His voice cracked. It was clear he retained a sense of shame. He had been given an order to detain me and to pin a charge of drinking and driving on me, without regard for whether he still harboured any of the self-respect that he would have to repress to carry out the order. He was not trying to persuade me so much as himself.

He became aware that he hadn't been decisive enough with me. He was through talking, he said. I'd been drinking and driving and therefore he was confiscating my driver's licence. The persons in the car would have to get out. I was to lock the vehicle, turn the keys over to him, and leave the car parked here until they decided what action to take.

I looked towards the car and saw a golden head of hair in the window. My daughter was anxiously watching a scene that would certainly stick in her memory far more vividly than better plays performed by better actors. Unfortunately, I was a performer in this play, and how I acquitted myself would also stick in her memory.

I said that no one was getting out of the car, that I would not give him my keys, and that I would lodge an official complaint about his behaviour.

'If you don't hand over your keys, you'll have to come with us.' His voice cracked again.

I didn't care about the keys. I learned long ago that a person cannot cling to objects if he doesn't want to become their slave. But is it the same with one's rights? If you don't cling to your rights, you will gradually be deprived of them, and become a slave all the same.

At this point the second uniformed officer, who had so far stood silently observing all this, moved. With a barely perceptible gesture, he motioned the first man aside and stepped into his place. He could see that I was upset, he said. People who are excited behave rashly. I should understand that at a time like this, it made no sense to argue over petty details. I had become involved in events over which neither I—nor he, for that matter—had any control. They had to take my driver's licence and keys. If I resisted, they would have to detain me, and they'd take my keys anyway and, given the mood that would prevail, I would certainly not be getting them back right away. What good would that do? If I surrendered the keys now, I could go home and go to bed, and when the dust had settled I'd get them back. He leaned over to me and said, almost in a whisper: 'Meanwhile . . . you have another set at home, don't you?'

I know that during interrogations the roles are usually divided. One of the interrogators plays the tough guy and the other one tries to gain the confidence of the detainee by kindness. But this was not an interrogation, and it didn't seem to me that these two had been assigned any complicated roles. They didn't have the basic props. They didn't have a breathalyser that normal breath would cause to change colour. They had not been taught how to switch a colourless tube for a coloured one. It seemed probable that the man who was talking to me now genuinely wanted to save himself some work, and me some unpleasantness.

But I still could not overcome my feelings of resistance and disgust. Should one submit to a false accusation only to avoid greater unpleasantness? If I acquiesced now, how could I later ask for justice?

It was my daughter who snapped me out of my indecision. She had decided, despite her youth, to whisper words of advice: 'To hell with them! Let them eat the stupid keys if they want.'

My friend the engine driver and admirer of Hamlet might have put it more subtly:

. . . Rightly to be great
Is not to stir without great argument . . .

We resist the One who, in various disguises, rules over us; we want to wrest from Her at least the right to the footprint we would leave behind, to the act we would consider our own. Our struggle for the right to a life of dignity is with Her. She and Her assistants, however, attempt to reduce to nothing everything the struggle is about, to transform a conflict in which everything is at stake into a petty squabble in which resistance seems the act of a clown.

When I handed the keys over to the more polite of the two officers, I asked him if he could at least give me a receipt of some kind.

'Of course, that goes without saying!' He seemed relieved to put this embarrassing interlude behind him. He took his notepad from his case, then hesitated. He asked me to bear with him and walked over to his car. A few moments later he returned. 'I regret to say,' he announced, without even looking at me, 'that I cannot provide you with a receipt for your keys.' I could learn, he said, about the fate of my keys at my local police station.

We managed to flag down a taxi. The driver wondered how two women in evening gowns had managed to find themselves on an empty highway. We tried to explain it to him, but he didn't seem to understand, much less believe us. At the detention centre, where we went after we'd changed our clothes, they looked at me suspiciously when I asked them to take a sample of my blood. The nurse looked at my ID for a long time as though she hoped to find a note there that would explain what had driven me to make such an unusual request.

I sat on a bench in a room with filthy walls covered with anti-alcohol slogans and waited for them to call me into the office. I could hear an incomprehensible shouting, and then two men in white lab coats dragged a struggling drunk past me, while a third orderly walked along behind them, ready to help if necessary. The drunk was spewing out obscenities and reeked of stale beer.

Ten years before we had been guests of the Presbyterian Church in Midland, Texas. Our hosts wanted to know what sights we'd like to see. We had no idea what we should look at, until it occurred to me that I would like to see the local prison.

What surprised us about the prison was its hospital-like cleanliness. Most of the prisoners were black, men and women, and they were kept in large cells. They were dressed in normal clothes; some of them lay asleep on benches, others stared at us with obvious hostility. Our guide, like all prison guides, praised the orderliness of the prison. He claimed that all the prisoners were prostitutes, or people arrested for being drunk and disorderly. Most of them, he said, would be released the following day.

We were living near the Canadian border; the journey to this spot had taken us three days, and the return trip took a day and a night longer. We covered about five thousand miles, staying at various hotels; we took a small boat over to Mexico, where we spent a day. When we finally returned home to the peninsula between Lake Michigan and Lake Huron, we realized something unbelievable: the whole time, no one had asked us for any identification. Not even when we visited the prison did anyone suspect that we might not be who we said we were.

They took a sample of my blood and told me that they would send me the bill, and the results of the test, by mail. When we returned by the night tram full of drunks, the streets were empty. Not a single yellow and white car was in sight, not a single uniform. The green day had ended.

Our car was where we had left it. My wife unlocked it with her keys, sat behind the wheel, and drove us home. No one followed us. Our street was dark—they'd turned off the electricity. Inside, we undressed for bed by candlelight. My first ball had surpassed all my expectations.

The following afternoon, when I left for the local police station, I was surprised to see a small crowd in front of the building where Mr Novak lived. They were gathered around the open hood of his shiny Mercedes.

'Come and look at this!' Novak called out as soon as he caught sight of me. 'I'll bet you've never seen anything like it.'

When he had got into his car that morning, the starter was dead. As soon as he lifted up the hood, he saw why: in the darkness of the night, someone had stolen his engine.

Why would thieves risk being seen or heard driving off with a stolen car? They would sell the engine for parts and no one could prove anything. 'They must have come here with a mobile workshop,' shouted Novak. 'And explain to me how they could have known that the lights would be off in our street all night?'

I asked if the police from the criminal investigation branch, or at least the local police, had been here to look for clues. I was naïve, he said. When he called them, they said they'd drop around during the day, if they had the time. As if I didn't know that better than he did. After all, last night they were out on a big campaign. Wouldn't I grant them even a day off to rest?

Even when they do come, said people in the crowd, they'll only record the theft for their statistics. A single stolen engine was not worth starting a formal search over.

As a matter of principle we never confiscate the keys to anyone's cars, I was told at the police station. Was I aware that I was committing a crime by falsely accusing an officer?

I returned home without my driver's licence.

My experience over the years had led me to two more contradictory conclusions. One said: what the strong take from the weak they will never voluntarily return. The second one comforted me: bureaucracy always has to take a case to its ultimate conclusion, so it can close the file.

My keys had to be lying around somewhere and soon they would be getting in someone's way. I decided not to think about them. I went out to prepare the garden for spring planting.

Not long ago I read that ten per cent of Americans believe the car is the greatest invention of all time, and another twelve per cent chose the wheel as the greatest invention, presumably thinking of car wheels.

I don't think I'd be a good American; I could get along very well without a car. I prefer to walk. I realize, of course, that a car is not simply a means of transportation. What we value about a car, sometimes even more than the fact that it goes, is the fact that it can be driven. In a world that is less and less driven by people, the car provides man with an opportunity to express himself more personally than he can in the rest of his life. As a driver, he can escape his everyday roles and responsibilities—or at least he can tell himself that this is so. Sitting behind the wheel, he is no longer a clerk, a deluded husband, an unsuccessful and insignificant city dweller; he is a driver. By driving, he becomes what he imagines himself to be. Instead of running in a dull and monotonous circle, he flies down roads to the unknown, towards ancient longings and phantoms. He flies down roads and becomes dangerous—through his dreams as much as his driving. That is why he must be stopped by the ever-watchful guardians of road safety.

When Martin the engine driver returned my books, he talked about crime on the railway. Trains would arrive at their destinations, he said, with only a part of their freight. It was understandable and even forgivable. When oranges disappear from a freight car, they may be the only oranges that people in that part of the country will ever see. But of course oranges are only the beginning. Once fifteen cars loaded with Wartburg automobiles were left on a siding, and several days later, just before they were dispatched, it was discovered that on the side away from the station, all the wheels had been stolen.

Martin had applied for a hard currency voucher for a trip to Denmark. As expected, he'd been turned down.

That evening Pavel stopped by to see me, his head still wrapped in bandages. He told me that several of our friends had been arrested on the way home from the ball, and no one knew what had happened to them. As usual, there was no mention of this in the media. We tried to tune in to some foreign radio station, but the jammers drowned out the announcers' voices. Jammers are the sound of a life that She—the one in disguise—directs according to Her notions. She knows that man has a notion of his fate and good fortune, that he wants to win, through his defiance, his right to his own footprint, action, sentence, to a truthful thought that he could declare out loud or at least hear expressed. But She is convinced that She and She alone can decide our fate; say what is good and what is evil. She desires that her sentences stay with us from morning till night, from the cradle to the grave, where one day She will lay us low. All voices other than Her own she brands false; they are banned and cannot be heard even from beyond the borders that She has ordered closely guarded. She has had the creaking of Her joints and the howling of the wind in Her empty skull recorded and amplified a thousand times. She orders that it be broadcast to drown all sounds of life.

Three weeks later the authorities sent me a message. I went to the local police station where the same young officer who not long ago had explained to me that my request for my keys amounted to the false accusation of a public officer now asked me impatiently why I wasn't taking an interest in my keys. Did I think that the police were some kind of baggage depository? I was to report at once to the commander of the special operations team.

The barracks of the special operations team was next to the street where I spent my childhood, so I found it with no difficulty. The commander of special operations was small and stocky, almost bald, and he wore glasses. His tunic was undone and underneath it I could see striped braces. He had a fatherly expression.

Yes indeed, he had seen my driver's licence, and yes, he even remembered that there were some keys with it. Three, wasn't it? Two? It was possible. One was bigger than the other. However, since I hadn't requested them for so long . . . it was now being dealt with at Vinohrady. On Peace Square. Did I know where the station was? Perhaps he'd better give me exact directions.

Behind him hung a large map of Prague and he backed up to it.

I said that for fifteen years I had driven around the square almost every day, and I was last there when the railway workers had held their ball.

Yes, that was right: the railway workers' ball, that would have been three weeks ago, wouldn't it? Well, the ballroom dancing season was just about over, and if I was going to go dancing—and he circumspectly let the word that had forced its way on to his tongue, slip from his lips—I would have to hurry. He offered me his hand. When I was already walking through the door, he asked again, with concern in his voice, whether I was sure I'd be able to find the station on the square.

The station was where it was supposed to be, but of course they had neither my keys, nor my driver's licence.

Crime was on the rise, even though the ballroom dancing season was coming to an end. The paedophile, whom no one was tracking down, was still at large in our area. A young medical student was raped and strangled on an international express train. And there were stories going round that the director of the automobile factory had given away, or sold for the price of scrap to influential comrades at least, a wagon-load of cars, which naturally did not belong to him.

I visited a friend of mine, a playwright who alone among my colleagues can publish what he writes and therefore has access to the comrades. He claimed that they had transferred the director to a less responsible position, and that things were beginning to get better. During my visit, a car stopped outside the house and a woman in gardening clothes jumped out.

As I understood it, the woman taught my friend's daughter. The clothes in which she arrived were emergency clothes. She had been wearing them when she returned from her cottage the previous evening—and now they were all she had to wear, for the time being. Over the weekend, thieves had burgled her flat. What they hadn't taken they had destroyed, systematically. They had pulled the drawers out of the cupboards and dressers and wrecked them. They had torn up her fabrics or poured varnish over them; they had burned her passport and bank-books and the parquet flooring, smashed her china, slashed her pictures. They had drunk her spirits, and what they didn't drink, they tipped over her Persian rug.

It was as though they were taking revenge on her for something, as though they enjoyed the act of destruction more than theft. The police guessed that there was a whole gang of them at work. The noise of the destruction must have been heard in the building, and her neighbours immediately beneath her and on each side of her were home all weekend, and didn't even come out of their flats to see who was making such a racket. What kind of people were they? The things the thieves carried off must have half filled a large truck. The tears in her eyes as she told the story were not only for the vandalism, but for the indifference of her neighbours, who did nothing to protect her property, and for the apathy of the investigators, who were unmoved by the wasteland her flat had become.

It occurred to me to ask what she taught.

She taught Marxism.

It didn't feel as though I missed being able to drive but oddly enough, at night, highways worked their way into my dreams with increasing frequency. I could read the names of exotic places on the road signs, or sometimes only the number of the roads that stretched through the prairies and clambered up mountainsides. The automobile was utterly unlike any I had ever driven; I was giving a ride to a girl utterly unlike any girl I had ever given a ride to, and I knew that we would make love as soon as I found an appropriate place. But could such a place be found on the highway? I turned on to a road that led into the woods, but that didn't seem deserted enough either; the trees were tall and widely spaced and offered no shelter, no real hiding place. I drove out of the woods and on to an empty plateau of sand. There was not a living, moving soul far and wide, and even the road vanished. I was still driving, and as the sand crunched and creaked under the wheels I felt the girl's naked body pressing against me. She had taken her clothes off during the ride. I stopped the car at last, hastily reclined the seats and changed the interior into a perfect bed.

As we were lying in an embrace I realized that the car, now driven by no one, had begun to move forwards. I raised myself up, and through the window I saw the edge of a precipice. We were moving towards it. I wanted to grasp the wheel and slam on the brakes, but the seats got in my way. There was nothing I could do. The car moved right to the edge of the precipice and I could see the depths below me. I screamed in terror, but no one heard me. I reached out for the girl, but felt only emptiness. She was no longer in the car, and I remained alone in my plunge into the abyss.

When I told the dream to my non-existent psychoanalyst, he persuaded me that the dream was not about how I longed to drive a car again, nor about how I desired to make passionate love to a strange woman. My dream was about the state of disinheritance in which I found myself. The girl symbolized the world beyond my family, the nearness of other people I craved for. At the moment when real danger appeared and the abyss opened up before me, the girl, the symbol of that distant community, vanished—what remained was solitude, which threatened to overwhelm me.

Two weeks later, I was invited to the Traffic Inspectorate where a short, slightly built major was sitting behind his desk. 'Ah, it's you,' he said when he had studied my summons. He leaned over and pretended that he was looking for something before he took a file that he had on his desk. 'Now I wonder how these got here?' he said, taking out my keys. He held them between his thumb and forefinger, raised them up with a look of bewildered surprise, and jingled them. 'I believe these are the keys to your car.'

He handed them to me and then began to study the documents in the file. 'My goodness, the things I'm reading about you here,' he said. 'On the evening of 20 February, one of our squad cars followed you along the embankment for a while, and between the Charles Bridge and the Iron Bridge you committed five serious breaches of the Traffic Act. At the National Theatre you even ran a red light.' He looked at me disapprovingly; perhaps he actually believed what he was saying. 'Our comrades also subjected you to a breathalyser test,' and he pulled the familiar tube out of the file, held it between finger and thumb and observed, as I had, its colourless state. 'The results, as you know, were negative.' He put the tube back in the file. 'Even so, the comrades justifiably held your driver's licence. Five offences—that's too many. Could you have been upset about something?'

He fell silent, as though he were awaiting a meaningful answer to his meaningless question. 'It happens,' he said. 'The driver may be sober, but because he's upset he can't concentrate, and instead of stopping and getting out of the car, he goes on driving and becomes a threat to other road users.' Once again he fell silent. When I still had nothing to say, he asked if I were willing to be re-tested.

I said I was, not to make his role too easy, and he gave me a form with questions printed on it.

'This is in order,' he said when he'd scanned my answers. He took my almost brand-new driver's licence from the file, grasped it and held it up as though it were something ugly, then opened it up, closed it again, opened it, looked at the photograph and then at me, and with distaste put it back in the file.

He said he couldn't possibly give my licence back to me in that state. Why the photograph didn't even look like me. I would have to apply for another one.

I asked him if, considering that the only thing at issue now was a new photograph, he could issue me with a temporary licence. But he was obviously so upset that he couldn't concentrate, and he didn't even appear to register my question. He stood up to indicate that our conversation was over.

When I got home, I found Martin the engine driver waiting for me. He had heard about my difficulties, and it occurred to him that the time had come for me to try driving a train. It couldn't be put off; at the end of the spring he was leaving the railway. They were offering him a place on a farm where he was to raise mink.

I told him that they were still hanging on to my driver's licence. That made him laugh. Wasn't that why he was here? Besides, as long as they had it, my driver's licence was worthless.

We left together, and got off the train in a small town in the foothills of the Ore Mountains.

We also long to drive so we can escape from Her. We step up to the driver's seat as if it is a royal (or presidential or secretarial) throne. It seems that we have dominion over the living and the dead. Overwhelmed by our own power, we succumb to the illusion that we have dominion over Her as well, since She could not possibly creep close to us and take us into Her embrace without our permission.

Once, far in the past, people believed those who ruled to be gods; later, it became clear that even they were controlled by a superior force; the same force that controlled everyone. It had the power of judgement and the knowledge of good and evil. Those who ruled must have known that they could only do so imperfectly; that they were stand-ins and that everything they judged would be judged in a higher court. But of course this didn't stop many from giving themselves over to the self-delusion and the intoxication that goes with power.

We talked for a long time, and it wasn't until midnight that I finally got to bed, in a bunk that was lined on three sides with books. I knew that we would be getting up at four and that then I would be entrusted with driving an engine about which I had no idea whatsoever. I couldn't sleep. I listened intently to see if I couldn't hear, from somewhere, the whistle of the trains of my childhood, but there was only the silence of a house in the country.

Next morning the darkness was so deep that it was still black when we got into a workers' commuter train that would take us to the station where our engine was waiting for us. The passenger car was crammed with sleepy men and women that duty compelled to go to work. We had to stand in the aisle. Did I understand the signals, at least a little, my host asked.

The language of lights, semaphors, grade indicators, detectors, markers, fishtails, order boards, wig-wags and targets, was something I had learned as a child. I hoped that an institution as conservative as the railways had not changed its language.

Very well, but he would test me all the same.

At the station we walked over to an engine that, now the possibility that I would actually drive it threatened, overwhelmed me with its size. My friend the engine driver had to go to the office for his working orders. He said it would be best if I hid behind the engine and didn't let anyone see me. He would let me in from the other side.

I was left alone. The station seemed deserted. The train we'd arrived on had gone, and the passengers had dispersed. A lone old man in a blue uniform with an oil can walked along oiling the wheels of the freight train. The tracks gave off an oily sheen in the light of the station lamps. The diesel engine smelled of kerosene. I walked around the train. Beyond the last set of tracks there was a steep embankment overgrown with shrubs. I sat down on an overturned stone bollard and waited. I was neither excited nor impatient; I had, after all, advanced well beyond the age when a man wishes to experience everything that excites him, just as he wants to make love to every woman he finds attractive.

Why, then, had I come here?

At that moment, the window of the engine lit up, then the headlights went on. A door high up opened. 'Come up, quick. We leave soon.'

I clambered up a steep set of stairs and entered the cabin.

'Do you want to change your clothes?' he said, and opened up a small locker. On the inside of the door I caught sight of some pornographic pictures accompanied by the dry commentary: 'Stop! Warning signal! Then all clear, all clear!'

I said that I didn't think I would change my clothes; I'd

rather he showed me what everything was for.

On the outside of the locker door, a blonde smiled on the shore of some lake, and next to her was a picture of Kronborg, Hamlet's castle:

The time is out of joint: o cursed spite,
That ever I was born to set it right!

There isn't much to show you, he said. It's easier to drive than a bicycle. But he showed me how to start the engine, and warned me that the half-wheel in the middle of the control panel wasn't a steering wheel, but an accelerator. It had eight positions and I would be controlling the speed with it. This was the emergency brake. The button next to the accelerator was called an 'alert button' and it would be my responsibility to push it once every ten seconds. It would probably bother me until I got used to it. Here was the speedometer. I would have to keep an eye on it all the time because the speed was registered on a tape and the tape was handed in after the trip. If we had gone over the limit anywhere, we would be fined.

He also told me that initially we'd only be hauling 320 tonnes, and would be picking up another eighty on the way. It wasn't a lot, but it was enough for those hills, especially if we had to get underway on a slope. Starting was the only thing that needed a little practice, so that the couplings wouldn't pull loose, or the wheels begin to spin. The first time, he would start himself. I would also have to realize that I was not sitting in a car, that 400 tonnes was a decent weight and when I was going downhill I should be careful not to go too quickly and fly off the tracks. And, when going uphill I had to make sure I didn't lose speed. As soon as I began to lose it, I would find myself standing still and I wouldn't even know it had happened.

At that moment, I noticed the signal ahead had turned from red to green, and despite myself I felt a twinge of excitement. 'Keep your head down for now,' Martin said, and leaning out of the side window he waved his hand to the dispatcher, turned the half-wheel slightly, and while I obediently crouched in a corner, we left the station.

The awakening countryside began to flow past us, but I

didn't notice it much, for I was looking at the speed signs; the speed limit here was low, and the whistle signals came one after another.

'You can take over now,' he said, turning to me and making room for me on the seat. 'Don't forget the alert button. If you want, I'll push it for you, for now.'

I said that I would try to press it myself. I sat down in front of the control panel, but the machine was not aware of this change. It was going by itself, as it was meant to do. The little light above the alert button came on at regular intervals, but I always managed to deactivate it in time, so that the machine didn't honk at me. The track began to rise gently and, mindful of my mentor's advice, I turned the accelerator a little. Thus we went through several stations, at least twenty level crossings, some with gates, some without, the motor rumbling regularly and the hand on the speedometer almost motionless. The speed limit varied from thirty to fifty kilometres an hour, and on the whole, I managed to accelerate or decelerate that enormous mass of metal smoothly. It was only after a while that I saw what an unusual view I had of the track unwinding in front of me, and heard the regular sound of the wheels clacking over the joints in the rails.

After an hour my instructor, who until now had kept a keen eye on the track, the engine, and my actions, took out his lunch, leaned up against the wall by the locker, and contentedly poured himself a cup of tea. More than any words could have done, his actions expressed his confidence in my capacities as an engine driver.

At one of the stations the guard came into the cabin and, paying no attention whatsoever to me, as though having a guest driver were absolutely normal, he began to talk about people I couldn't have known, one of whom was a colleague who got so drunk on duty that he couldn't even stand up, and was in that state when an inspector found him.

The story interested me, but at the same time I couldn't really listen, though I gathered that nothing happened to the drunken engine driver; he had faked an acute attack of lower back pain, and who would dare be so cruel as to compel a colleague suffering from excruciating pain to submit to a breathalyser test?

It seemed to me that the two of them were enjoying themselves and not paying any attention to the track, but suddenly my friend called out, 'D'you see them? Now you can blow your horn at them.'

It was then that I noticed, at the level crossing we were approaching, a yellow and white automobile with the widely ridiculed letters on it.

'If only they could see you like this,' he laughed, 'those brothers of theirs, the ones who hung all that nonsense on you.'

I gave a blast on the horn. Perhaps I actually caught a glimpse of Her at that moment. At least I thought I saw Her sitting there: all bone, her favourite disguise, grinning and showing her teeth at me, while I flashed past. Now I was aware of those tonnes I was controlling, and I saw the wagons behind me in a bend in the tracks and I succumbed to the illusion that I was pulling them along with my own enormous power. I had crossed Her path.

'Can you brake a little? We're going downhill anyway,' he reminded me.

I understood why he had invited me, offered me the opportunity, for a moment at least, to cross paths with Her, so that I would know I was not battling Her alone.

'You forgot the alert button,' he said immediately afterwards, reproachfully.

In an instant I returned to my place and pressed the button, as a sign that I was still alive.

Translated from the Czech by Paul Wilson

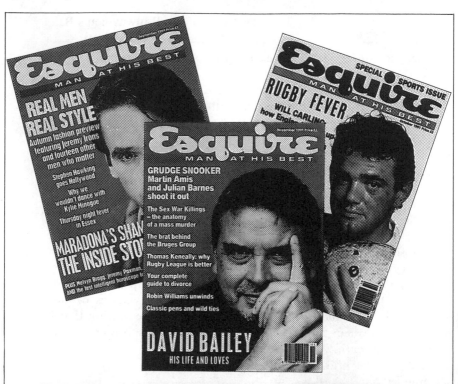

Wit. Ideas. Style. Good Writing. That's Esquire.

Tracy Kidder
The Adjuster

On the day my career at Fireplace Mutual began, six of us recruits filed into the smoke-filled office of the Supervisor of Adjusters, Mr Kreisky. His office smelled like the inside of an old taxi-cab. There was nothing on the walls. I remember feeling disappointed. I wanted *my* boss to have a fancy office. Mr Kreisky sat in shirt-sleeves and necktie behind a large, grey, metal desk. I expected someone who looked well-fed and at least a little jovial; someone fatherly. Kreisky was maybe fifty-five or sixty. It was hard to tell. He was very lean and leathery. He had pock-marked cheeks and bony-looking shoulders, and he didn't have much hair. He had a way of narrowing his eyes and staring at you until you felt uncomfortable. The minute I saw him sitting there I had the feeling he'd never met a person he liked or was afraid of.

Kreisky didn't get up to greet us. He didn't offer to shake hands. He sat back and looked us over slowly, one by one.

I felt very lonely standing there, waiting for my turn. I wore my best suit, and I carried a brand new fake-leather attaché case. I didn't have anything to put in it, but I had thought it lent me the right touch. Kreisky's eyes lingered on it. 'What you got in there, your lunch?'

He looked at my face. I smiled at him, to show what a great sense of humour I had.

He sneered back.

Maybe I just looked ridiculous to him, a boy trying to dress like a tycoon. But I think there was more. I come from people who haven't been oppressed, except by their own kind, since 1066. I have their straight, narrow, pointed nose, and, I guess, their superior look. I'd learned to smile with this boyish geniality of ours, which seems to say to some people, 'I don't need to compete with you.' Besides, I wear glasses. Just then my mouth was probably hanging open. My new boss hated me already. I was on the verge of smiling some more, and saying that I didn't have anything in the attaché case now but I sure hoped it would be filled with work by the end of today.

But Kreisky had finished examining us. 'Welcome to Whiplash City, boys. I'll be seeing you around,' he said. He went back to his paperwork, and we filed out past his secretary, who held the door.

137

Tracy Kidder

W e spent most of the next week in a conference room at
school-type desks, a week of studying pie charts to give
us the big picture of the industry and of reading the
company rules and of filling out make-believe accident reports.
Late on the first afternoon Mr Kreisky came through the door of
our classroom, tall and lanky and stoop-shouldered, dressed in a
loose, grey, slightly shiny suit, trailing cigarette smoke and ash.
We were expecting him. The instructors had told us that Kreisky
would give us our lectures in auto-claims adjustment theory.
     Kreisky went up to the podium. I got ready to take notes.
Then Kreisky told us this was a subject that couldn't be taught. 'I
was an adjuster thirty-eight years, boys, but I don't know what to
tell you because you learn adjusting in the field.' And to my great
surprise, he walked away. He stopped when he got to the door
and said to us over his shoulder, 'So let's go get some coffee,
huh?'
     Silly as it sounds, this performance left me feeling grateful.
Kreisky had relented. He'd try to help us after all.
     Kreisky sat at the head of a table down in a far corner of the
basement cafeteria, and we sat half-turned in our chairs to face
him. 'OK,' said Kreisky, 'the first rule of adjusting, you never get
to know for sure what happened in an accident.'
     He seemed to be waiting, but no one spoke. I saw a chance.
'How come?' I asked.
     He gave me a little nod, and said, 'How come? Because the
light was always green for everybody.'
     I bowed my head and made an entry in my notebook, feeling
thrilled and slightly guilty, as I'd felt in early school days the first
time I successfully brown-nosed a teacher.
     Kreisky's raspy voice cut in on my thoughts. 'And you need
to know about whiplash. We have a whiplash epidemic. Any of
you know what whiplash is? Actual whiplash?'
     I wet my lips. I meant to personify attentiveness.
     'Whiplash is a person standing on a corner and a car goes
by. He gets a stiff neck from the wind.'
     I nodded, hoping he would notice. I wasn't just brown-
nosing. This wasn't school. This was preparation for my life.
What Kreisky introduced me to in the cafeteria on the first days

138

of that week was reality, I felt. I'd never known the world contained so many greedy and deceitful people, bad drivers and victims alike. I decided I admired Kreisky. Obviously *he* knew how to get along in that place he called 'the field'.

'OK. Women,' he told us. 'Women lie the most, and the best. She takes out a couple of hydrants parallel parking, she makes up a story to tell her husband, and by the time you show up to get the facts, she believes her own bullshit.'

I made notes on most of what he said, knowing that I'd need all the tips he was willing to offer, when I had to go out alone to the field. He referred to that place at least once every session, sighing and saying again, 'But. You learn adjusting in the field.'

Thursday in the cafeteria began with Kreisky warning us about the lies victims would tell when we came to make our pain and suffering estimates. Kreisky slouched in his chair. My classmates slouched in theirs, stirring their coffee with candy-striped sticks and wearing little crooked grins modelled after Kreisky's. I'd copied that grin myself sometimes. Just then I had put on what my father used to call 'the look of eagles', which he admired in a young man. I looked straight at Kreisky, showing him how serious I was—how strong my chin, how tight my lips. I'd been doing this all week. Then his eyes locked on me, and I had to drop mine. I looked down and made notes on what he'd said: 'Pain and suffering. Compute, then subtract at least twenty-five per cent.'

Training ended tomorrow. All of Thursday's session I worried about next week in the field. By the end, when Kreisky had relaxed into his story-telling mood, I felt worn out from the strain of trying to mask my worry, and little by little, I guess, I let down my guard. 'This was, Christ, thirty years ago,' Kreisky began. 'I told you boys about assigned risks, right? The psychos we *have* to insure? We had 'em back then, too. This one mowed down some old dozer. Our client's in the wrong. Of course. I think he ran his car up on the sidewalk and hit this old guy. The claim's gotta run fifteen, twenty grand, which was big money back then. My supervisor, this was going to make his books look bad, he says, "Kreisky, show me some smarts." So I sit down and go over the file. I realize that this guy our client ran over is from

139

the old country. Right off the boat. So I tell my supervisor, "Kreisky's going trick or treating." He gets five hundred out of the safe. In singles. I had dollar bills sticking out of my pockets like handkerchiefs. That's a fat roll, five hundred bills, if you got it all in ones.'

He took a long, deep drag on his cigarette, and his words came out surrounded by smoke. Watching the smoke drift out of him, like steam through holes in a street, I thought, 'Oh, God, what's trick or treating?' Was this another skill I needed for the field?

'So I go see the old dozer. I say, "My company wants to do the right thing. We want *you* to tell *us* what we owe." And I whip out that roll and I start laying down babbit, one dollar bill at a time. "Now you tell me when to stop," I say. Pretty soon he starts talking to himself. By the time I get to two hundred he can't take it any more. He tells me, "Stop! Save-a some money for the other people that get in accidents."'

I heard someone chuckle. I looked at the other fledgling adjusters. They were smiling. I bit my lip. I wanted to ask Kreisky if he expected us to be able to do something like this, right away, out in the field.

'I felt kind of sorry for him,' Kreisky was saying. He shook his head, smiling back at his memories. 'Yeah, I hadda put another fifty in the pot. And, you know what? Everybody was happy. The old dozer, he was happy as hell. My supervisor was so happy he gave me a cut of the rest of the five hundred. Which made me happy. What's *your* problem, champ?'

I had turned away. I'd been running my finger along the grooved mortar joints in the concrete-block wall beside the table, thinking, I could never pull that off.

'You got a problem, champ?'

I turned and looked around the table and saw everyone staring at me. Looking at Kreisky—the grey hair too thin to hide his scalp, the pin-holes in his cheeks, the lines of sneer around his mouth—I thought that I could see the early stages of his life. It's amazing what you can see in a hostile face when it's aimed at you. I bet the other kids made fun of him, I thought.

'A bleeding heart. They sent me a fucking bleeding heart,' he said, staring at me. 'You want to clean out the company safe paying off on whiplash. Huh?'

I felt limp. My mouth felt dry. I looked at my lap. I'd taken more notes than anyone. I'd asked more questions. The injustice of this!

Kreisky said, 'Yeah, I think you *would* clean out the safe.'

His voice sounded different. I raised my eyes. He still stared at me, but in a way that looked more curious than angry.

At that moment my life began to change. I realize now that Kreisky had decided I was innocent, when I was really just naïve.

2

The next day, the last day of training, the instructor handed me a note that said to report to Mr Kreisky's office. On the way I rehearsed a speech. It started, 'You got me wrong, sir. I don't mind tricking people . . .' Even in my mind this sounded odd, but I meant it. I didn't want to get fired before I'd even started work.

Mr Kreisky told me to close the door and sit down. Then he said, 'I need a bleeding heart. Lucky for you.' He sat back in his orange vinyl office chair, which had patches of tape on its armrests, and talked about Albert Einstein for a while—the gist of it was that he'd heard somewhere how Einstein flunked geometry in school. Smiling his thin smile, he said, 'In claims, you're looking at one of the people that flunked geometry, Bleeding Heart.' He sat up. 'So listen.' He added, 'Don't take notes. Just listen.'

'The company insures a person. This client commits an inexcusable act behind the wheel. Maybe the client gets drunk, runs a red light, and kills a child or a pregnant woman. The client's policy is worth, say, 100,000 dollars. The victim's family wants it all. The company offers 60,000 dollars. The victim's family retains a lawyer, on contingency. The case goes to court.

'You should hear our attorneys. The light was yellow. The victim didn't have both feet inside the pedestrian lane. Feeble, OK?' said Kreisky. 'The jury doesn't buy it, and company ends up paying the whole hundred thousand. But who gets it? Here's the catch. The victim's family takes home maybe sixty thou. If they're lucky. The attorney takes expenses and then another thirty-three. Minimum.'

Did I follow him? I nodded. Could I imagine a better way? I shook my head. But Kreisky knew one. 'What if we keep the attorney out of it and give the family eighty per cent? The victim's better off. Obviously. And we save the company twenty points a whack.' Was twenty points a lot of money? I wasn't sure. Well, of course, it was a lot. 'Some of these people insure their car for a million,' he said. He muttered, 'They shouldn't drive a bicycle.'

It seemed like a good time to offer a compliment. 'I guess it takes a lot of experience to figure all that out, Mr Kreisky.'

'Kreisky,' he snapped. He was rummaging in a desk drawer. He glanced at me and sniffed. 'Everybody can figure it out, Bleeding Heart. But maybe they don't have any reason to do anything about it. Maybe they don't know how to keep the attorney out of it. You ever think of that?'

'No, sir.'

'You want to see some smarts, you listen.' He had taken a bulging file folder from his drawer. Holding it in his lap he swivelled in his chair a quarter turn, so that he looked at me from the corner of one eye, and he said, 'I got good adjusters here. I don't need a *good* adjuster. If I sent out a good adjuster and he offered these people a *hundred* per cent, a lot of them wouldn't take it, they'd go to an attorney.'

Kreisky's office had a window. Through it I could see a patch of the Expressway, a stream of cars. He gazed out that way, too, and went on, saying, 'Today, most of these victims are suspicious. *And* they feel sorry for themselves. You should like this job.'

He turned and tossed the fat file across his desk. I caught it as it was sliding off the edge. IMPOSSIBLE CLAIMS was stencilled in red on the cover.

Kreisky had immersed himself in paperwork and wasn't looking at me. Somehow I sensed that he couldn't look at me and give me the advice he did, as I headed for the door. 'You gotta be you,' he said. 'Be nice.'

Kreisky's secretary showed me to a tiny office. I guessed it used to be a janitor's closet. Behind the desk above my head a bar was still in place and a couple of old hangers, which I didn't dare remove at first, clanged together softly when I typed reports.

All the other claims adjusters did their desk work out in the loud, metallically furnished hall they called Whiplash City. I think Kreisky meant to isolate me from my peers, who might soil my valuable innocence. He didn't need to bother. I didn't belong to the ordinary world of adjusting. I wasn't assigned the kinds of cases that the other adjusters joked about around the coffee machine: the whiplash frauds in rented neck braces, or the pedestrians whose minor bruises became compound fractures, through the magic of snap-on casts, when adjusters visited.

I dealt with bereaved parents and children and spouses, and once with a young widower whose honeymoon began and ended on the same car ride. Visit a victim and hear a sad story, that was my routine. 'And then everything stopped and it sounded like, you know, the telephone was ringing . . . ' 'I'm saying everything's OK, I'm going to be all right, and then I realize I can't feel my toes. Holy cow! I can't feel my toes!' 'The first we heard was from the coroner. Why us? Our little boy. He was just a baby and they had hung the curtain out for him.'

People who have lost something they can't get back, like a limb or a teenage child, don't want money just for itself. They need it as a symbol of the worth of what they've lost. Sometimes they want revenge too, but they always want dignified money, not pay-offs. Thanks to Kreisky's plan I didn't have to insult the victims by negotiating with them, or by applying the pain and suffering and earning power formulas. I sat on lots of sofas in stunned households and did what came most naturally. I looked sadly at my shoes and listened. These people, so suddenly and extremely bereft, could read in my silences whatever they liked, and usually what they read was what they knew they deserved, which was true sympathy. I'm sure that's what I felt at first.

I almost never raised the subject of cash settlements. Sooner or later the victims would do that. Then I'd offer them, per Kreisky's instructions, eighty per cent of the reckless (who should be locked up but at least were insured) drivers' liability coverages. To some, but never loved ones, who were most likely to feel guilty, I explained about the lawyers. Some victims already knew that I offered the better deal. A few got angry with me. They said, 'Where do you get off, who are you to be telling me what my leg/arm/son was worth?' Then I sat and listened some more and looked miserable, at first because I felt that way and later on also because I knew that this approach usually worked.

By mid-winter, after several months on the job, I had worked out with the company's computer centre a system that brought me ahead of attorneys to the doors of a statistically significant, increased number of impossible claimants. Around the coffee machine, the other young adjusters talked about the lawyers they contended with. In lowered voices they swapped rumours about the 'brief-case bums', also known as 'brief-cases', the lowest kind of lawyers, who tried to bribe adjusters to settle bogus claims. Whenever an adjuster got fired the gang around the coffee machine would whisper that Kreisky caught the guy taking kickbacks from a brief-case.

I was tired listening to that kind of talk. 'Look,' I told my colleagues the first time I dared to argue. 'It isn't always like that. Real accidents do happen.' As time went on, I talked more. I told some of the stories I heard in living-rooms. For a while they listened. I'd hear them cluck, I'd see them twist their lips. Believing I was reaching them, I got bolder. 'Yeah,' I said. 'It's terrible out there on my beat.' Eventually, real talking seemed to stop when I came out to join them for coffee, and then one day when I had finished telling them about a case of decapitation, a claims man piped up, 'So you could say this guy *lost his head* over a little old car accident.' The other adjusters and a couple of the secretaries burst out laughing, the long and too full-bellied laughter that people share, when someone finally says what everyone has worried that he alone had felt. I stared hard at the wise guy and then I walked away. I punished them by drinking my coffee alone after that.

But I needed to talk shop with someone. Usually when I

applied for an audience, Kreisky would tell his secretary through the intercom, so I could hear, 'Go ahead and let him in. I already have a stomach-ache.'

I would sit down and tell him about my cases. Usually he would keep on working, muttering now and then over his paperwork. Eventually he'd say, 'OK, get out of my life.' Once he said, without taking his eyes from his papers, 'You're doing a good job, Bleeding Heart. And you're revolting me.'

'I care about these people, Mr Kreisky,' I retorted.

'Kreisky.' He made a face over his document. 'Yeah? Well, it's a good technique. So keep it up. Goodbye.'

I tried other subjects that I thought would interest him. 'Kreisky, are there really a lot of these brief-case bum people around?'

That time he at least looked at me. 'Where'd you hear about that?' he snapped.

'Just rumours,' I said.

He went back to his papers. 'I don't have time for rumours. *Or* sob stories, Bleeding Heart.'

I'd never had an accident myself, but a time came, after about six months, when I would be in my company car, driving away from another unhappy household, out in the huge, paved suburban plain, and although I could swear I'd never actually been there before, I would suddenly recognize a place or a situation. This, where an on-ramp interfered with an exit, was a dangerous clover-leaf, and that five-way intersection was a tragic one. I'd glance in the rear-view mirror and seeing a car tail-gating me, I'd think of spinal injuries. Or up ahead a car with fat tyres and its rear end jacked up like a beast in heat would dart across three lanes without even signalling, and every muscle in me would flex and my fingertips would tingle. Up there, at that exit ramp, would another confused old man use it as an entrance and meet *me* head-on this time?

On secondary roads, I'd travel a mile out of my way in order to avoid left turns. I felt edgy whenever I turned on to the Expressway. Around the office they called it Double Indemnity Road. If I had to go that way, I made sure I came back before three, so I would miss the evening traffic from the city.

'Kreisky, when you were an adjuster, did you get sick of driving?'

He grunted. He was busy, always busy with his files, when I came to talk.

'I feel like a doctor for these people,' I continued.

He grunted again.

'But I'd rather be a doctor. A doctor doesn't have to worry all the time about catching what his patients have on the way to work.'

He looked up at me. 'Now you feel sorry for everybody. Congratulations.' He went back to work. 'So? Go away. See a rabbi, see a priest, go back to college. Leave.'

I was only twenty-two and far away from home. I lived by myself in one of those suburban apartment buildings that are named for what they have replaced. This one was Fox Hollow. Most of my neighbours were couples and I had the impression that they spent their free time arguing—the building's walls were thin—and waxing their cars. I slept a lot and watched television and imagined my neighbours wondering about me, a young man going places that they would never visit. I didn't have any friends, but I had many imaginary admirers, who whispered about me and guessed that I was doing something brave and good. If someone in the building had made the slightest overture, I would have chattered for several days straight, but when I came out of my apartment, I moved briskly, even when I wasn't in a hurry.

I never even took the trash out of my company car. It had filled up, front seat and back, with road maps folded every which way, stained styrofoam coffee-cups, old newspapers and discarded accident reports. I felt proud of my car's squalor. It proved that I was different. The trash rose and fell in the Expressway breezes pouring in the windows. It was spring.

Around lunchtime one sunny day, heading back from a home visit on one of the safer, less heavily travelled secondary roads, which traversed a run-down neighbourhood, an early suburb gone to seed, I saw Kreisky with a woman. I was stopped at a light beside a place called The Four Seasons Bar and Grille. I glanced out the driver's window and there they were, standing together, talking and laughing about something, near the front door of the cocktail lounge.

I don't know if I'd have noticed her if she hadn't been with Kreisky. She wasn't much older than me, I guessed. She was robustly feminine, short and stocky with sturdy calves and a delicate snub nose. I imagined I could see her father in her. He would be a big, good-looking man in a lumberjack's coat. She wore her hair pulled back into a simple bun from which a few curls strayed, as if by accident, to dangle over her ears. I stared at the swell beneath her blouse and inwardly applauded. She wasn't the best-looking woman I ever saw, but I remember thinking that she'd be good-looking enough for me.

I gaped out the window. I didn't notice the traffic-light change. The driver behind me hit his horn. Kreisky turned. He saw me staring at him and the woman. He scowled. He put his arm around her. Ushering her in the door, he went on scowling at me from over his shoulder.

I drove back alone towards Whiplash City. How did Kreisky find a girl-friend like her?

I had a new case file in front of me and some parents to visit. Kreisky scribbled words on the top pages of files he sent down the hall to my 'In' box. 'Violins' seemed to mean a sad case, for instance, and 'hearse' meant an ordinary fatality. These were notes to himself. Once in a while he wrote a note to me. The one on this case file said, 'You can jack off over this one.' I had read the contents. We adjusters used to call these 'velvet curtain cases': an only child; female; motorcycle passenger. She'd have wrapped her arms around the insured's waist and leaned her cheek against his back, so if nothing else, she must have smelled alcohol. I looked at the last picture of her. In the picture she had tried to smile like a movie star endorsing dentistry, but she had a porcine face and her front teeth were splayed.

A pathetic case. I was stalling. I wanted to avoid my company car for another hour, to let the morning period of breath-taking lane changes and sudden stops on Double Indemnity subside. I was sitting at my desk in the janitor's closet, with the door ajar, and I wouldn't have minded if someone had come by for a chat. I put the victim's picture back in the file and closed the folder, and I started doodling with my calculator, trying to put numbers to idle questions. How much gas did the company's adjusters use in a year? Out of the Expressway's sixty-eight miles, how many feet had never seen blood? How much money had I saved the company adjusting this impossible claim, adjusting that one? I got lost in that last calculation for maybe fifteen minutes. I didn't keep a running tally. I was saving up the total as a surprise, a mathematical dessert. Press the memory button, press addition, repeat—it was sort of fun—and finally a number spread across the little grey screen that I held in my hand.

I got up from my desk then and went to my door. I looked down the hall, both ways. But no one was loitering there. Out across Whiplash City, the secretaries and adjusters bent over desks and leaned their ears against telephone receivers. A paper airplane floated across the hall. I closed my door and locked it, and I did the calculation all over again. I had known I was successful in the speciality Kreisky created for me, but I had never looked at it in terms of money before.

A few months after I had started visiting accident victims, around the time when I had started calling them my clients, I took down the closet bar and hung a small mirror head-high on my office wall, to see how my face looked when I felt sorry for a stranger. What had disappointed me in mirrors—a variety of ordinariness (a girl I liked once described me as 'nice-looking') had begun to seem like an asset in my office mirror. This face got the job done, after all. I grinned into my mirror now, alone in my office, with the door locked. I had done well by my clients, and even better by the company. Five hundred thousand and change saved in impossible claims so far, I figured.

And no one had given me anything for it, no raise, no new office—I would have been grateful for a room large enough to turn around in—not even a thanks from Kreisky.

Well, I thought, as I watched myself straighten my tie, this company was about to make a charitable contribution to some clients of mine, and if Kreisky didn't like it, he could fire the best adjuster in the company.

Driving into suburban developments I no longer noticed much except for numbers on doors and lamp-posts. But driving up to that ranch house that morning, I saw everything, the little lawn, the bird-bath, the tidiness of the little house—they must have washed their aluminium siding regularly—the shrubs pruned to geometrical shapes, all the things that made this house different from the other identically-planned houses on the block. And it occurred to me as I pulled up that the accident that had severed the people inside from their child was about to forge a new connection, not just between us but between me and a new life of noble purpose. I hurried up the walk. I had to remind myself at the door not to look too cheerful.

The father sat rigid, in an easy chair, looking straight ahead. You had the feeling he hadn't moved since the news came, and that he might not ever move again. 'Life gave us the finger,' he said to me, but he could have been talking to himself.

The mother talked to me. I was ready to speak for a change, but she didn't give me a chance. She was ready to be angry. 'One. Her pain and suffering.' She glared at me. 'Two. Her earning power. She got straight As, mister.'

Obviously, she had already talked to an attorney, or else she had a friend in insurance. 'Look,' I said, 'This isn't necessary.'

'You let me finish!' she said. 'Three! Our investment, mister. We invested everything we had in her.'

Then, maybe because she remembered some things she wished she had bought for the girl—the child in the picture could have used braces, I thought—the mother started weeping. She sat on the edge of the sofa, hands cupped around her face.

It occurred to me that I could argue the facts. The girl probably died instantly. So much for pain and suffering. As for earning power, a sixteen-year-old hasn't got much. But I had come to heal, not argue. I stood up. 'You people are in pain, and I care about that,' I said. 'I know money's not the real issue. But what is insurance for?'

'Life gave us the finger,' the father muttered. The mother wept on. I wasn't sure I had an audience.

'What is insurance?' I began again. 'It's knowing accidents will happen, but not knowing where, and it's a lot of people

149

contributing to help the unlucky ones go on.' I liked the sound of my voice just then. I made it stronger. ' "Just give 'em eighty per cent, and less if they're easy." That's what my boss says, but I'm through with that. I'm not giving you eighty per cent, I'm not giving you ninety. I know it won't bring her back, but I'm giving you the whole thing.' I strode across the room and dropped the documents in the father's lap, the standard documents, executed by me as usual, but carrying new kinds of numbers. The father just stared at the bundle, and the mother kept on sobbing, but it was a thrilling moment for me. With my help, they signed, of course.

I thought about Kreisky all the way back on Double Indemnity. He wouldn't know what I had done until next Monday when he got this week's paperwork. I had four cases that week, an average load of tragedy for me. On two of them I handed out one hundred per cent, to some nice, grateful people. On the fourth case I bargained the next of kin down to seventy per cent. I didn't like his attitude. 'You blew it with me, pal,' I said, driving away. I felt free and strong and right as Solomon.

The following Monday I came in early as usual, ahead of the worst traffic, and waited at my desk for Kreisky, who always came in on the other side of rush hour from me. I felt too jumpy to read the new case histories in my box. I felt fragile in my stomach, but I didn't wish I could undo my last week's work. Obedience and safety were all behind me now. Then Kreisky's stoop-shouldered figure appeared in my doorway, and he smiled at me, smiled with most of his teeth, and I wasn't so sure.

He closed the door behind him. 'Been having fun, Bleeding Heart?'

That really irritated me. That heated up my courage. 'I'm not doing this for fun, Kreisky.'

'No?' he said. 'Well, whatever, you can't do this. You can't give away that money, pal. It doesn't belong to you.'

'So who does it belong to?' I said. 'The company? I don't care about the company. A company doesn't have feelings. I care about these people, Kreisky. They're my clients.'

'No,' said Kreisky evenly, and through his teeth. 'It belongs to *me*.'

'Huh?' I said.

He hovered over me. I should have stood up right away.

'Today you stop handing out that money. I'm not going to have you screwing everything up just because you feel sorry for yourself.'

'Go ahead and fire me,' I said.

He had grown very calm, it seemed. 'I don't need to fire you yet. I'm going to give you another chance. If you actually care about your *clients*, pal, if that's what this is really all about, you better make your settlements at eighty per cent. Think about it, Bleeding Heart.'

I thought about it the rest of the morning. If you looked at it from the company's side—and the company was really just people, so the money I'd given away did belong to Kreisky among others—I'd cheated everyone inside the company last week. And if I kept it up, I'd injure my clients, too, by getting fired and not being there to help them realize they preferred eighty per cent from me to sixty per cent from an oily attorney.

One hundred per cent was too immaculate a figure for anyone to deserve. Who could say what anyone actually deserved? Kreisky's eighty per cent was a pretty generous average, and eighty per cent without exceptions was the fairest formula. It was the best I could do. I felt sorry. I really did. I started to explain all this to the victim I visited that afternoon. But that victim—he sat in a wheelchair; he'd sit there for ever—looked puzzled, and I stopped. I told him that money couldn't cover losses like his, but that this money, this eighty per cent, came as a fumbling apology from a world of imperfect drivers. He sat back in his chair and said, 'What?' I handed him the papers. He read, glancing up at me now and then, as if I were a potential mugger on the other side of a street. He signed.

A few days later, a few days of obedient, eighty per cent settlements, I came back from one of my house calls and found an envelope on top of the files in my 'In' box. There wasn't any writing on it. Inside I found a packet, about an inch thick, of crisp twenty-dollar bills.

3

If someone gives you money that doesn't belong to you, you should give it back right away. You could keep it. You might not even touch it at first. You might leave it in its envelope in your top desk drawer, to give yourself time to think about what you should do with it. But if it keeps on coming, you get used to it, and if you're in a line of work where you meet unfortunate people and you give them some of it or buy them something with it, you figure that's all right, because you're not using it for yourself. But you do have your own personal needs, and if you're helping other people, then after a while you realize that helping yourself is really the same as helping them. You might have a job that takes a lot out of you but doesn't pay well. You get used to eating out and having some nice clothes. If you don't inquire, you don't actually know where it's coming from. You might imagine a wealthy philanthropist who's heard about your work, or a boss who secretly admires it.

Of course I knew all along that Kreisky was paying me for obedience, and that spending his money made me someone different from the person I'd imagined. Now I was letting Kreisky decide who I would become. Or maybe I'd already made that decision myself, and he'd simply discovered it. Once he'd found out about those glorious one hundred per cent settlements of mine, he'd probably known that I was corruptible.

I tried not to wonder why the payments came in cash. I stayed away from Kreisky's office. He stayed away from mine for about a month. An envelope arrived each week. On a Monday morning in early June, I looked up from another bloody case history and saw Kreisky coming through my door. He closed it behind him. He tossed another envelope on my blotter, and sat down on the edge of my desk. 'I'm taking you to lunch, BH,' he said. 'You should know where it's coming from.' He smiled down at me. 'I figure you already have a pretty good idea.'

He had changed his name for me. I wished I had my old insulting one again. 'I'm going to pay it all back, Kreisky,' I said.

'Nah.' He waved away my words. He closed his eyes half-way, and nodded gradually, surveying me. You know what you're turning into, BH? A real fucking A insurance adjuster.'

We went to that restaurant-cocktail lounge, The Four Seasons Bar and Grille. It was always dusk in there, the kind of place where you can't see the carpeting and know that you don't want to. 'Some joint, huh?' said Kreisky, when the three of us were seated in our booth. 'There's a lot of Four Seasons restaurants. But in this place, you know what the seasons are?' He gestured at the television alight above the bar. 'Baseball, football, basketball and hockey.'

She laughed. A little too loudly and too long. I realized that right then, in the corner of my mind where I kept my self-restraint, like money in a shoe. But when she turned and smiled at me, I didn't care. 'I laugh at all of Kreisky's jokes,' she said. 'He doesn't know that many.'

I'd liked her from across the street. I liked her better now. We ordered. She had salad. 'I think they aged my lettuce,' she said, staring at her dish. A moment later, the harried waitress scurried by and asked, 'How is everything here?'

'Atrocious,' Kreisky said.

But she smiled at the waitress. 'Just ignore him. It's fine.' When the waitress had left, she said to Kreisky, 'OK, big shot, you better leave her a good tip.'

'Yeah, yeah,' said Kreisky.

'I used to be a waitress,' she said to me. 'Then I got into banking, but I had to quit.'

'She cleaned out the safe,' said Kreisky.

'No!' she said to me. 'I was a teller. You had to say have a nice day to every creep like Kreisky who walked up to your window, or else they docked your pay.'

'So now she works for criminals,' said Kreisky.

She smiled at me, ignoring him. 'How about you? How do you like insurance?'

'Oh, fine,' I said. I didn't know where to begin.

'Kreisky says you're a genius.' She put on a deep voice. 'The genius of the impossible claim.'

'He's learning,' Kreisky said.

153

'Of course,' she said. 'And from the old master, Mr Smarts.'
She laughed and reaching across the table, patted Kreisky's hand.
Kreisky cracked a smile. Then he said to her, 'OK, Babe, it's
getting late.'

She had two voices. Talking business, she was brisk and
serious. At first I couldn't understand a lot of what she and
Kreisky said. They shared a special language, which made them
seem like intimates and made me envy Kreisky. Her name was
Louise. He usually called her 'Babe,' and once 'Beneficiary' in a
way that made me realize significance lay behind it. She called
him 'Larry'. I never thought of him as having a first name, or of
there being someone in the world who would feel inclined to use
it.

'Whattaya got this week, Babe?'

'Well, first of all, two whiplash.'

'Who from? Ponies? You know what's wrong with him? I'm
serious. No imagination. Five grand each, that's all.'

'Maybe ten on one of them? He has a doctor for it.'

'This is Mr Pills, I bet,' said Kreisky. To me, he said, 'The
guy's a drug addict.'

He looked at me for an extra moment. I nodded. I knew I
was supposed to. Kreisky had promoted me in his estimation. He
expected me to understand. In fact, I had begun to. Louise was
what was called 'a getter' in the trade, working for a bunch of
brief-case bums. She brought Kreisky their phoney insurance
claims—inflated claims for minor accidents, claims for accidents
that had been staged, claims for accidents that had never even
happened but which a degenerate doctor might verify for a fee.
And Kreisky paid out company money to settle these bogus
claims. She got a percentage of the pay-offs. So did Kreisky. So
did I—since about a month ago. I wanted to ask him some
questions right then. Like what part I had in all of this, and why
he wanted me to know he was stealing from the company. But I
didn't want her to think I was naïve. So I just nodded. And they
went back to dickering about the size of that week's pay-offs.

'She's crazy about me,' Kreisky said as we walked back. 'She says she wants to marry rich. I told her the hours are too long in that business. She works for deadbeats, but she's smarter than them. I'm not easy, BH. I took out some policies, but I'm not putting too many in her name yet, until I see if she sticks. I made it worth her while. You know what I'm saying?'

'You took out life insurance and made her the beneficiary? Does that appeal to her?' I said. I wasn't thinking. I just blurted it out.

'Yeah, well, like I said, she's crazy about me,' retorted Kreisky.

He didn't look at me. I could tell he didn't want to discuss that any more. And for just a moment, and really for the first time since I'd known him, he seemed like an old man to me.

Two days later, Kreisky wandered into my office again. 'Lunch, BH.' He stopped in front of my practice mirror and gave his thin grey hair a run-through with a comb, which he produced from a hip pocket. He stood with his knees a little bent, combing with both hands, like an old drugstore cowboy. He parted his hair only an inch or so above one ear and flipped it across his head, like a threadbare knitted rug draped across his skull. Combing and patting, he said, 'Hey, BH, when you take your vacation, you should use your company car.'

'You can do that?' I asked, because the rules book forbade private use of company vehicles.

'I know somebody. He turns back odometers. He's a pro. You take the car on a trip and later you get him to fix the mileage. I'll give you his number.

But what if, I thought, I had an accident while I was on vacation? I wanted to say no thanks, but then I noticed Kreisky's slacks. He had finished with the mirror and sat now, one knee bent, on the edge of my desk. In the trouser leg of his grey suit, just above the knee, I saw several holes, each about a pencil lead's diameter, with neat, blackened edges where fallen ash had cauterized the plastic in the cloth. I felt confused. This seemed like secret knowledge. I can't say why, but I felt I had to accept the odometer specialist's number.

He seemed pleased. 'Listen, kid. You can't get anywhere in this business. The only thing you get is what you take from the bastards.'

We ate lunch together twice a week and sometimes more the first half of that summer. Sometimes Louise joined us. She'd always say something pleasant to me, like, 'Nice suit, BH. This old cheapskate give you a raise?' I would feel excited and talk too much. I always felt an increase of blood pressure when she appeared in the gloomy restaurant, bare-armed in summer dresses, but if Kreisky noticed, he never spoke to me about it.

Usually he and I ate alone. He'd pay the bill. He wouldn't eat much. As near as I could tell, he nourished himself on coffee and Danish and unfiltered cigarettes. We always went on foot, out of Whiplash City, across a shadeless landscape of concrete and asphalt with office buildings and a department store in the distance across vast parking lots, then over a bridge that spanned Double Indemnity, waves of traffic passing below us and thinner streams around us. One time Kreisky said he could remember when all of this was potato fields and open spaces intervened between the villages, so you could tell what town you were entering without reading a road sign.

'It's too bad,' I said. I guess I thought he was showing me a soft spot.

But Kreisky said, 'you're still about half full of bullshit, you know that? What do you know about growing potatoes?'

We walked along, the pavements so hot at those midday hours my feet felt scorched. We must have made a conspicuous pair, a couple of lone figures in suits, one tailored and one shabby, the only pedestrians anywhere in sight, surrounded by cars and delivery trucks and trailer trucks and utterly alone outside, as if we were on an arid planet and only we could breathe the air. Gradually, buildings grew less distant. When we finally struck old-fashioned sidewalk, we were in a remnant of a town, whose windows were mostly bandaged in plywood. Always we would turn into The Four Seasons, and Kreisky would lower his voice and grow laconic. He did his talking on the way, shambling along.

Among adjusters he had been—or so he told me—the most

productive and most cunning in the history of the company, and when they'd made him supervisor for all auto claims, the officers had let him think that pretty soon they'd make him one of them. 'The officers,' he said one time. 'They talk like you, BH. They pronounce the *g*s at the ends of words, all right?' He made them seem like interchangeable men, with mahogany desks, closets full of fine blue suits, unlimited expense accounts, and four cars each.

For years he'd waited for the call. Finally he had asked for his promotion. I could hardly imagine that, Kreisky going begging to the Home Office. The officer in charge of personnel had told him sorry, it wasn't possible, Kreisky wasn't officer material. 'Yeah, bullshit,' Kreisky said to me. 'You want to know the real reason? They don't trust a good adjuster. They think he'd steal the safe.'

I could see how Kreisky might have created that impression. I'm not sure that Kreisky could. He had other theories. He told me once, 'Those guys think an adjuster doesn't have the smarts. Now I'm giving them a demonstration, right, BH? And they don't even know it. So who's so fucking smart?'

We were walking along the edge of a parking field. 'Any moron in this business should know to be careful with his books, BH. But I did better than that, didn't I? Yeah, the real beauty of this thing, BH, is you.' Kreisky eyed me, wearing a squinty grin. 'And you didn't even know that for a long time, huh?'

I smiled back. 'I gotta hand it to you, Kreisky.' I was still a step behind him. That night I got out my calculator and it finally dawned on me. The company had expected to pay out the 500,000 dollars that I'd saved in impossible claims this year. That meant Kreisky could do 400,000 worth of business in bogus claims through Louise, and, leaving the other 100,000 in the company's account, he'd show a net reduction of 100,000 in total claims payments for the year. Our officers cared deeply, I expect, about total claims payments. If that total had gone up by 400,000, they'd probably have arranged a surprise party for Kreisky with the Special Auditing Department. But if the total fell by 100,000, they'd probably send Kreisky a case of Scotch. The next time we walked to lunch I tested my hypothesis. 'So did the officers send you a present yet?'

'Not yet.' He wore his crooked smile. 'But I figure I might get a raise. On top of the one I already gave myself.'

Kreisky had distributed most of the 400,000, through Louise—and only through Louise—to the various brief-case bums and their clients and the doctors in this game. Businesses always brag about providing jobs. Just on the side, I figured, Kreisky was providing livelihoods for dozens of other people who might otherwise have done worse things. For himself Kreisky had stolen, via kickbacks, about 30,000. And he'd given me about 10,000 of his share. And what did Kreisky do with his cut? He didn't buy new clothes or a car, or go to horse races. He bought insurance. Whole-life mostly, a trust fund, so to speak, for Louise. He never told me why he bought Louise insurance instead of jewellery, but I thought I understood. He'd worked in insurance all his life. He *believed* in insurance. He was a pessimistic man.

Walking past wide parking fields with Kreisky those hot summer days, I often thought about my part in his scam. He had made me his confederate long before I'd realized it. The work I did had always been legitimate and it still did some people good, both my clients and the company. So what if I got paid partly in stolen money? I had tried philanthropy. Maybe philanthropy is safe if you have religion and believe you're following orders from God. Personally, I think you're in trouble the minute you believe you're doing good. Then you congratulate yourself. You get pleasure out of helping unfortunate strangers. Pretty soon you're glad that other people get in accidents. I felt cleaner knowing that I did my job partly for money Kreisky stole. I just hoped we wouldn't get caught.

On the Thursday after the Fourth of July, I sat at my desk staring at a stack of new case histories. Kreisky walked in. He never knocked. He glanced at the stack of files, said, 'Holiday drivers. Why don't they just shoot each other?' and gave his profile a quick check in my mirror.

'Kreisky,' I said. 'Sometimes I feel like quitting.'

'Hey,' he said. 'This is the busiest it gets. You'll get over it.'

'It isn't that,' I said. 'I'm scared.'

He patted his hair-do into place, and said, 'Nah, you're

bored.'

But I was scared, and I was lonely—mainly thanks to him. I felt like quitting, but I felt like quitting everything, not finding a new job. Besides, saying I wanted to quit clearly worried Kreisky. So I kept it up.

Well, did I want a raise?

I shrugged.

Why not take a girl-friend to the beach?

I shook my head. 'I don't know anybody.'

He shook his head at me. 'Stop being pathetic, BH.'

This went on for a while. Then one night Louise called me at my apartment. Wasn't this heat brutal? She was taking tomorrow off. She'd like to go to the beach, but her car was in the shop, and Kreisky wouldn't drive her, he hated the beach, he said it was overrated, you might as well swim in a storm sewer and you didn't have to drive as far. He'd told her I'd said something about going to the beach myself. She'd like to hitch a ride. Could we take my company car?

After she hung up, I went out to the parking lot with a flashlight and tried to clean the car. At least I made the passenger seat habitable. I stayed up half the night cleaning my apartment too, just in case she wanted to see it.

Alone in bed the past month or so, I had often conjured her up. I wished I could see her bedroom. I bet it smelled good. I'd watch her tie back her hair and strap herself into a dress in the morning. A dress on her was like a sweet concession to femininity. 'I'll be really nice to you,' I'd say to the ceiling, while in my mind she told me, 'I really like a man in glasses.'

We went to one of the state parks on the south shore and lay around on towels in our bathing-suits. I could have measured the distance between our towels to the nearest micron and drawn with my eyes closed the exact curvature of her breasts, so snugly contained in the enviable cups of her bikini top. Lying on our stomachs, our chins on our hands, we whispered about the physiques of bathers passing by. 'Hairy gorilla,' I offered. She giggled. 'Saggy tits,' she whispered back. When she said to me, 'You've got a good build, BH,' I must have blushed again, and examining those words in my mind, I thought happily, 'I bet

159

Kreisky doesn't.'

Walking down the beach in the evening, dodging the day's crop of broken glass and empty beer cans and soiled plastic diapers and agreeing to be indignant about the slovenliness of 'people', we made, I felt, a world of two. I felt my body glowed like hers. We were made of precious radium. For what seemed like forever I tortured the question 'should I try?' At last I touched her hand, as gingerly as if I'd touched a wound. Right away she laced her fingers among mine, and I felt suddenly benevolent towards everyone, including litterbugs, and I declared, 'Oh well, I guess people don't know any better.' And yet even at that moment her manner troubles me. The way she'd taken my hand—she'd agreed to that too easily, as if it didn't signify a thing to her. She seemed much older than me. She seemed like an older sister, or—it couldn't be—like a babysitter.

Louise didn't come back to my apartment. When I dropped her off at hers she gave me a quick kiss on the cheek. Her hair brushed my face, I got a whiff of sweet lanolin, and then she was gone, a vision of hips swinging through the doorway. I kept reinventing the tingle of that kiss and felt like crying the next morning when I had to shave that cheek.

I saw Kreisky's girl-friend occasionally. I didn't say anything to Kreisky about it. When her name came up I acted nonchalant. I'd say, 'Oh yeah? How's she doing?' When she wasn't around he often referred to her as 'the Bosco'. He'd say, 'I have a meeting with the Bosco. You want to come along?' I'd feel like punching him. I would go along, though. I'd sit staring glumly at my food while he and Louise talked business.

I wasn't making much progress with her. She never invited me to her place, and I couldn't figure out just the right way to ask her back to mine. She didn't want me to ask her. I could feel it. I'd had girl-friends back in school, but I didn't know much about women. I still assumed that most of them liked earnest men. I told her about my cases. I said life wasn't fair and something should be done about it, and that was why I worked so hard on the impossible claims. One time I told her all about my brief rebellion and how Kreisky had defeated me. 'He's such a bastard,' she said, but she was grinning. Usually she just listened to me. And listened some more, her elbows on the tables of the fancy restaurants I picked out, bracelets dangling at the ends of decorous arms, and the more I talked, I think, the less interested she was in me. One night, trying to find the words to ask her back to my place and not finding them, I asked her to marry me. Deranged as I was, I must have figured it amounted to the same request.

She laughed. She said, 'The hours are too long at that business, BH.'

That was Kreisky's saying, the one about marrying rich. 'But I'm not rich,' I blurted out.

'That's what I mean,' she said. Then she reached out and held my hand for a moment, and said, 'Thanks anyway, BH.'

I walked around with a hard-on half the time, thinking about her. I bought her flowers and jewellery and dinner at restaurants where I'd tell her I was scared about being involved in Kreisky's scam and might have to quit my job. I couldn't tell any more if I was scared. If she thought I might quit, she might sleep with me, in order to save her business. Maybe she figured the opposite—that if she slept with me I might not have any reason not to quit. Anyway, telling her I was scared got a rise out of her, and I couldn't break the habit. She'd say, wearily now, that even if the worst happened, Kreisky wouldn't rat on me. 'He isn't like that.' One time she said, 'Look at it this way, BH. If he gets caught, you might get his job,' and she smiled and made her eyebrows dance.

'Would that change things? You know, between us?' I asked—unusually direct for me.

She shrugged.

Finally, one evening late that summer, she put a stop to my whining. I was saying, 'You know, this really gets to me. It's scary,' and she leaned over the table and said, 'I like smart crooks. I'm not interested in someone that doesn't have a spine.'

Afterwards I paced around my apartment until about midnight. I had to call her. I'm afraid I woke her up. 'This is BH. I'm going to change.'

'I hope so,' she said, and hung up.

I called her back. I couldn't help myself. But this time a man answered. 'Hell-oh.' It was Kreisky. I never heard anyone answer a phone the way he did, cursing you in the first syllable and declaring in the second that he was already tired of talking to you. I hung up.

I called her the next morning from work. She agreed to dinner but said she'd come in her own car. We sat down and I confronted her. 'You let Kreisky stay at your apartment last night.'

Her nostrils flared. She said, 'I never told you I'd stop seeing Kreisky. But I'm going to stop seeing *you!*' And she walked out.

The sight of the office building at exit 41 made me sad, but I preferred it to my apartment, where dishes filled the sink again, and to my company car, where the passenger seat was always empty now, except for coffee cups and wadded up accident reports. I stayed in the building after hours and even on some weekends, sometimes doing paperwork but more often wandering among the desks of Whiplash City and standing at the windows that looked out on the Expressway. The windows didn't open. I guess that was just as well. I'd gaze out at blue skies and billowing clouds and remember my first bicycle and my aching, boyhood dreams of travel—down an endless country lane in the sunshine, forever moving on. Leaning against the window frames, I'd study the traffic on the Expressway. Occasionally, I'd see an accident in progress out there, and like a housewife at her sink, I'd realize all at once and over again that this job of mine would never really end and never really change.

I often thought about them. Kreisky naked would be skinny, with loose flabby dead-grey skin. Ashes and roses. She'd kneel on top, breasts triumphant. He'd lie under her wheezing. But I wasn't so sure. Imagining them copulating didn't make me less interested in them—in either of them.

Kreisky had become for me the kind of circumstantial, stopgap friend that many children keep to fill the space between their better friends. He was company and the nearest thing I had to contact with Louise. Maybe he would talk to her about me, and if he did I'd want him to report on how I'd changed. I'd begin by letting Kreisky know that I wasn't afraid of being involved in his illicit business any more.

He visited me in my office more often now, since Louise had dumped me. I remember one visit, on a Friday in early August, an empty weekend looming. He asked how I was doing. 'Terrible,' I said.

He turned to the practice mirror and combed his hair, his back to me. I think he found it difficult to look at a person when he had something pleasant to say. 'You couldn't handle a claims department yet,' he said, flipping that thin mat of hair across his bald crown. 'You couldn't handle the paper-clips. I mean, don't get me wrong, but nobody else could do this job you're doing. So. You want a raise?'

I'd felt this way when I'd rehearsed my lines in that mirror before going out to settle a claim: as if I starred in my own movie. Only now it was Louise and Kreisky watching. 'Yeah, sure,' I said. 'Why not?'

4

After you work a while in claims, you believe the accidental is normal. In the last hot days of fall, two weeks before our routine audit, the abnormal happened. I came to work and didn't find any new files on my desk. Only one new case came in that week. By Wednesday I'd emptied my 'In' box. On Thursday I had nothing to do, and sitting in my stuffy tiny office, I began to reinvent my fears, maybe just to make the pain of missing her subside. Something was wrong. Something was impending. I analyzed my situation. I hadn't done anything illegal. If Kreisky's scam unravelled, the most the officers could do was fire me. They couldn't get me sent to jail. Not unless Kreisky had a plan for dragging me along with him. Or for laying the entire blame on me.

I found my 'In' box empty Friday morning. I went to Kreisky's office. He lay back in his swivel chair, his feet up on his desk. He was looking out his window at the late morning traffic, cheering on the drivers, so to speak. 'Jesus Christ! You see that? Luckee!'

He turned to me. 'Quiet. You know it. This happens. It goes on too long and the Home Office starts looking for something to do, we might have a problem.'

'What kind of problem?'

'Scared you, huh?' Kreisky laughed a little, his bony shoulders shaking. 'Nah.'

He went back to window gazing. 'I saw this a lot of times before. We call this hurricane warning time. Lookout. Better get ready for overtime. You know how many psychos we got out there, BH? You think they all decided to go to Drivers' Ed last week?'

'Are you holding out on me, Kreisky?' I said. The minute I said it I didn't believe it. But I wanted reassurance. 'Are you getting ready to sell me to the SAD or something?'

Kreisky glanced at me. He shook his head. He sighed. 'You gotta know when to be suspicious, BH. How would I sell you to the SAD? Why the fuck would I, huh?'

All the same, I knew something important was about to happen. Maybe it was the impending audit. If you worry as I do and think you are receiving warnings from the future, and the worst doesn't happen, you know that your worrying prevented it. But if you worry all the time, you're bound to be right once in a while, and when that happens it comes as a terrible shock, and you think you didn't worry enough. I was addicted to worry.

My apartment and the inside of my company car were filthier now than before Louise. I never balanced my chequebook any more. I took my clothes to the laundry, in a great smelly bundle, only when I got down to my last shirt. I put gas in the company car after the needle dropped into the red. Now, not having any work and lots of time, I couldn't bear the thought of doing something insignificant, like paying my overdue rent or stopping at the cleaners. I came to work the next Monday with a dirty collar. My 'In' box was still empty.

Kreisky poked his head in my doorway around noon. 'The Bosco called. She wants a meeting. She wants you to come.'

She wanted to see me? Maybe she's going to dump him, I

thought. Maybe this is the day she tells him she's realized she wants me.

Everything was as usual, the dusky bar-room, the booth in the far corner, the sticky table-top, the smell of public toilet cleanser. But she sat there dressed in a suit. She looked ten years older, and she had on her business voice. She merely nodded to me.

'I have some cases for you, Larry.'

'Hey,' he said. 'I got an audit coming. You know we don't do business now.'

'That's *your* problem, Larry,' she said.

'No. It's ours,' he said. 'What's going on here?' You could tell he was sincerely puzzled. I was only disappointed. I wasn't nervous about this meeting yet.

Then she said, 'Actually, Larry, I don't care what you do. The investors care. I don't.'

He looked at me as if to say again, 'What's going on here?' I shrugged. He looked at her. 'What investors, Babe?'

'I started an organization.'

'Yeah?' He smiled then. 'Like a brief-case bum association? You going to join the Rotary? So, what is this, you sold them shares in me?'

'Something like that.'

'Babe, that's pretty good. Did you sell them a piece of the Expressway, too? I'm proud of you. No, I really am.' He laughed, and then coughed for a while. 'So that's why I haven't seen you for a while? Listen, it's OK.'

But she didn't smile. 'I didn't want to have to tell you this,' she said, and, of course, I knew right then that she'd rehearsed her lines. 'But you don't have a choice. It isn't up to me. My investors will insist. Business as usual today, ten per cent more next week.'

'No way.'

'They have some tape recordings, Larry, and some documents.'

'Tapes?' he said. 'What, you and me doing business? You made some tapes and sold them to those creeps?'

She smiled. There was nothing sweet about it.

'The documents don't worry me. I never showed you anything important. The tapes could be a problem. That wasn't very smart, Beneficiary.' He spoke that name slowly, pausing over every syllable, his elbows on the table, his face as close to hers as he could get it.

She stared right back at him. I felt proud of her, staring him down that way, but she'd begun to scare me too.

'They wanted some collateral, Larry baby. They paid me pretty well.'

'What else did you sell them, you whore!' I'd never seen him overcome with anger before, the veins in his neck popping out. His manner always threatened anger. The real thing wasn't as frightening. I actually felt sorry for him, for about five seconds.

She flinched. In the gloom her neck glowed red. I thought that she looked beautiful aroused. 'You thought you could buy me. You think I care about your life insurance policies? You'll live too long for that to pay me back.'

'I got you started,' Kreisky said. 'I taught you everything.'

'Exactly,' she replied.

'You're just another getter. I overestimated you.'

'No,' she said. 'I'm not. That's what this is all about. You try to buy me with those stupid policies, and then you use me as bait for this poor kid. What did you tell me to do? Let's see if I remember, Larry. "The kid's a basket case. We gotta keep him happy. Show him a good time, but don't let him in your pants." You didn't say that, Larry? I think you did.'

I glanced at Kreisky. I caught him shaking his head at her—telling her to keep quiet about that. So she'd wanted me there to hear this, to get even with Kreisky through me.

'No offence, BH,' she said to me. 'I think you're sweet.'

What about exciting? What about interesting? Wasn't I interesting at least? 'I'm not so sweet,' I muttered.

But she'd gone back to work on Kreisky, who stared at her with his lips pursed, just taking it. 'I want you to understand this, Larry. If you did that to me, I had to wonder what came next. I saw a chance for a little financial independence. I'm not a bosco, understand? I'd like my apartment key, please.'

'I'd like the tapes,' he said.

I might beat him up, I thought. I probably could.

'Be that way,' she said. 'My landlord would like the key, but, hey, I'm leaving town tonight.'

'You aren't leaving town?' said Kreisky.

She got up. 'You can talk to your stockholders tomorrow. They'll be here at noon. OK, Larry baby?'

'Thanks a lot, Kreisky,' I said.

He said, 'Thanks for trying to steal my girl.'

'You set the whole thing up, you bastard!'

'You couldn't find one by yourself.'

'Well, you can stay out of my personal life, Kreisky.'

'Fine,' he said.

'Fine,' I said.

We walked along a while, the only sound besides the traffic Kreisky's laboured breathing.

After a while I heard him say, 'Do you believe that?'

'What, Kreisky?'

'What she said about the policies. How can she not care about insurance policies, huh?'

We kept on walking. After another quarter mile or so, I asked him the question that had lodged in my throat. 'So what are we going to do?'

'About the tapes? I don't know. I don't think her *investors* would sell them to the company. They wouldn't get that much. But maybe they don't know that. These people aren't too smart, or they'd be real attorneys. I have to talk to them. Don't worry. They got nothing on you.'

'But *you* do, Kreisky.'

He stopped and faced me. I wonder what the passing drivers made of us, a pair of men in dark suits on hot asphalt, glaring at each other.

'I don't think you should talk to me that way, BH,' said Kreisky.

We started walking again. Our building hovered in the distance across the parking fields, which had turned into a lake. It kept receding as we walked on side by side.

5

Kreisky didn't get back from lunch until late the next afternoon. I'd waited for him for hours in my office, unbending paper-clips. Right away I noticed his necktie. He had unbuttoned his collar and pulled down the knot of his tie, the way homeward-bound businessmen do, bragging about what hard days they've had. Kreisky never let down his guard that way, and it made him look old and exhausted, as if he'd been struggling to get out of a noose. I don't think I'd realized how much I counted on Kreisky. I didn't like to see him looking this way. He closed the door and sat down above me on the corner of my desk. 'We got a problem, BH.'

This was what being scared felt like—like something interfering with my breathing. I'd only played at this before.

'I should have seen this coming. I go over there and there's five of them for Chrissake. A scumbag convention.'

I looked up at Kreisky. He wasn't looking at me. He slowly shook his head.

'First thing they say, they want to know am I holding out on them. So I tell them, look, I got an audit coming, I don't do their kind of business now. And they say they understand that. That's why they came up with this great fucking plan. Know what it is, BH? A three-car wreck.'

'Oh, no!' I said.

'Yup. A three-banger. They got this put together already. Three cars, all pros with policies. They tell me this takes care of my problem. This is legitimate business, a real accident, and they control the whole thing. And if they like this one, they can maybe do a bigger one next week. Yeah, sure. These guys are pros, but you can't control a thing like this. Some old dozer comes cruising along in the middle of this thing of theirs, and you know what we got, BH? We got a good shot at being involved in a homicide.'

The week's envelope of kickbacks lay in my top desk drawer. I didn't care about her any more. I didn't care about him. I had to get rid of that envelope before the auditors arrived.

'Listen, Kreisky,' I started.

He turned his face towards me. 'Excuse me, BH, I'm not finished, OK?' I dropped my eyes. I still couldn't stare him down. He lit a cigarette.

'So what I did, I acted like, hey, no problem, this accident's a good idea. Then I ask them where's it gonna be, what time? Because I don't want to get anywhere near this thing, I say. So one of them tells me, "So don't go home on the Expressway eastbound around six." Then I say I hope the pros have the mechanics figured out, and another one of these brief-cases says I don't have to worry, the pros are getting together around five to figure out how they're going to smash into each other. And I say I hope they picked a safe spot and this idiot says yeah, they're meeting at Josephine's, the bar next to exit 46, which I'm sure you know, BH.'

I knew the exit. There was a badly designed on-off ramp situation there, which caused a lot of real accidents.

'So we have to drive out there.'

'Drive?' I said.

'Yeah, BH. We drive to Josephine's and tell these psychos it's called off, no accident tonight, try again next week.' He crushed his cigarette on my floor. 'I think we have to stop this thing. Don't you?'

I didn't know what I thought about that. He was supposed to make the decisions.

Kreisky turned to my mirror and worked on his hair. I opened up my top desk drawer and took out the envelope. It was of fine rich heavy paper, the best company stationery, like the envelope that carries a wedding invitation. I used to love the texture of those envelopes. I could throw it away on Double Indemnity.

When Kreisky opened the passenger door of my company car, he paused and stared and in a voice that sounded impressed he said, 'Jesus, BH. This is revolting.' With a lot of rustling, he cleared a place to sit.

It was early evening, the sun in my eyes, when we pulled out into the traffic. Kreisky sat with his knees practically up to his chin and started talking to the drivers around us, sometimes yelling at a passing car: 'Slow down, yo yo!' Sometimes speaking worriedly: 'Come on, lady, use your blinkers.' Sometimes pleading softly: 'Chrissake, please don't pass me on the right.'

So Kreisky was afflicted that way, too. In sympathy I drove ten miles an hour under the speed limit. 'Take it easy, champ,' he said. 'We got time. Don't drive so fast.'

We passed exit 43. Our goal was 46. We ran out of gas between 43 and 44.

Out on the vast black road it had just begun, the great hour of returning home. Kreisky didn't bother with recriminations. When all is said and done, he had a philosophical temperament. We stood beside the car in the breakdown lane, our trousers fluttering in the hot gusts from the road, our hands in our pockets. 'We could hitch-hike,' I said.

'I don't know,' said Kreisky, 'I never did it. One of my adjusters told me a story about this hitch-hiker once. Hitch-hiker gets in and goes half a mile and he figures out the guy who gave him the ride is plastered. They go another mile and this driver's getting excited, yapping away, and he pulls off the steering-wheel. He's holding the steering-wheel and it isn't attached any more. Can you imagine that? So he looks at this poor hitch-hiker who's sitting there, and he says to him, "I'm getting outta here," and he rolls out the door. The hitch-hiker survived. It was a pretty big settlement. Anyway after I heard that story, I figured what the hell, maybe somebody's trying to tell me something. You want to walk?'

A tow truck had pulled into the breakdown lane behind us. It didn't come right up, though. I waved to it. 'Oh, yeah,' said Kreisky. 'These guys.' I started walking towards the tow truck. They could sell us gas. The truck backed very slowly away. So I turned around, walked back to the company car, looked behind me, and there was that tow truck advancing back to its former spot.

'Come on,' Kreisky said. 'If we walk fast, we still got time to talk the psychos out of it. Come on, you like to walk.'

I didn't want to leave my company car to that tow truck. I hated the car, but it was a place I had suffered in.

'Come on, BH. Let 'em have it for Chrissake.'

We hadn't gone far when looking back, I saw the tow truck's yellow lights blinking. Moments later it went by us out on the road in the right lane, with my car half aloft in its wake. Gradually, it passed out of sight.

I felt all alone out there. Have you ever walked along the banks of a busy highway? It's a lost world, a bone-yard really. People leave important things out there: letters, pets, neatly tied up plastic bags you'd feel afraid to look inside. Pieces of vehicles rust in the weeds. The place belongs to crows mostly, the way garbage dumps belong to gulls. Crows know where to look for death. They sauntered away as we approached.

Kreisky took long strides, lips narrowed like a bottle end and breathing musically, a sound that might come from behind a curtain in a hospital room. We didn't talk. He needed all his breath for walking. He strode on down the highway, suit coat flapping, the long shock of hair on the left side of his head streaming upward. He was all brilliant grey in the evening light.

I hurried along beside him. At footspeed I noticed how, every few feet, the guard-rails were dented. I noticed tyre tracks on the walls of a bridge abutment we passed under and tried to remember if that was one of my accidents. And the faces inside the passing cars, most of them looked *bored*. I felt all worried out, and the calm that comes from walking. My mind had cleared.

Kreisky had a lot of weaknesses, I thought. Probably he'd try to get back together with Louise. She wouldn't let him. But if she did, I thought, he'd better cancel those insurance policies. Or else he'd better be careful what he ate.

Kreisky was a romantic. He believed that only one or two people in the world could do certain jobs, which allowed him to flatter himself and think he had the gift for picking those specialists out of a crowd. He thought me irreplaceable, but that was only because agreeable manners were alien to him. I figured anyone with some good early training in etiquette could have adjusted impossible claims.

On the highway headlights came on. We'd passed exit 45 when we heard the sirens.

'Look out, Kreisky!'

I grabbed his arm—it felt as thin and lifeless as a stick—and pulled him after me, out of the breakdown lane and over the guard-rail. In a moment, two police cars shot past. An ambulance was working its way through the traffic out there. We stood behind the guard-rail in the grass, the sirens growing slightly fainter and the sound of Kreisky's panting growing fainter too. After a while I heard him say, 'Too late, BH. Let's get outta here.'

We climbed up a grass embankment to the access road. From up there to the east I could see a circle of red and yellow flashing lights. They looked pretty in the distance.

'Well, BH, we tried.'

He seemed to think I was upset. But to tell the truth, that accident out there meant nothing to me. I wasn't in it. I think Kreisky cared more about it than I did.

EUGENE RICHARDS
PHILADELPHIA

The 'War Zone' in Philadelphia is just north of the centre, about a mile and a half from City Hall and across the street from Temple University. The War Zone takes its name from the fact that most of the people who live in it are armed. Most—grandmothers, children, whole families—are also involved, on some level, in the only business driving the local economy—crack and heroin.

Eugene Richards made two trips to the War Zone. The first was in the autumn of 1989, and he was there for six weeks. He returned the following year, during the summer, and is about to re-visit the area some time this winter. During his first visit, he witnessed three people dying on the streets; their deaths were unnatural ones and were the result not of police brutality or of gang shootings but of the killing strength of the drugs available: the people who died were heroin-addicts from the suburbs, unused to pure heroin, deadly heroin, the only heroin sold in the War Zone.

Although the United States is committed to a campaign against drug use—both in its own cities and throughout Latin America—there is little evidence of any such campaign in Philadelphia. The policing here is inadequate and underfinanced, and most officers enter the War Zone with the greatest reluctance. The photographs that follow illustrate a police visit.

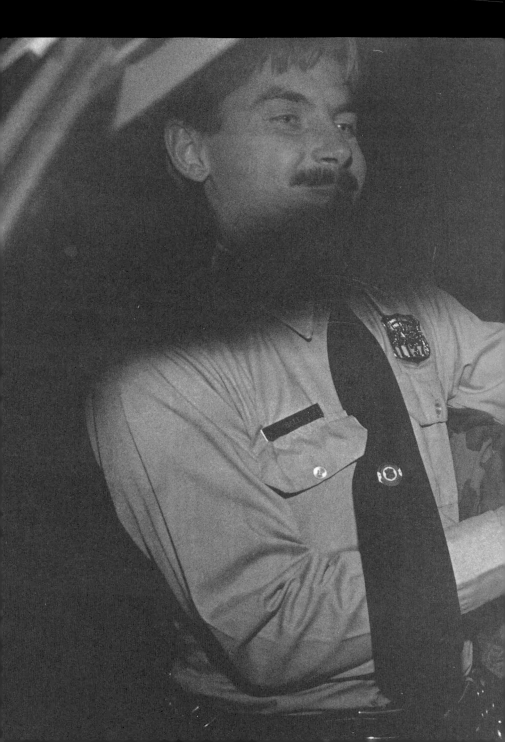

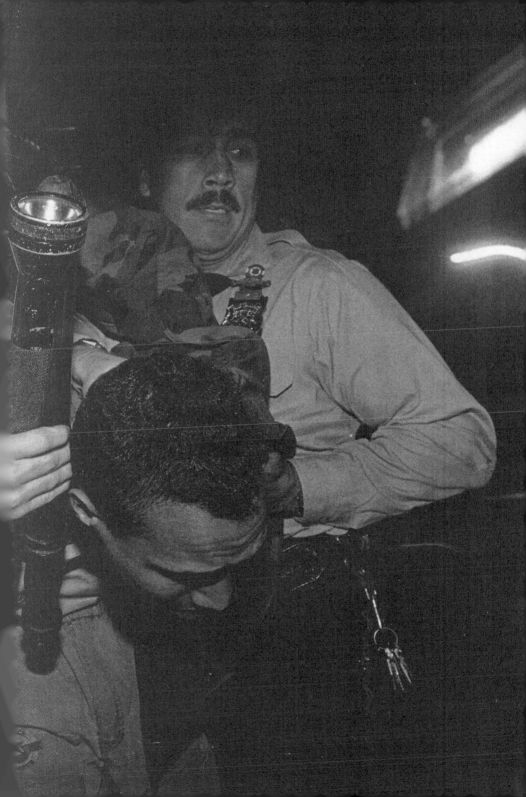

JOHN UPDIKE

Rabbit at Rest

The fourth and final novel in John Updike's
triumphant *Rabbit* tetralogy

LOUISE ERDRICH
NIGHT PRAYER

It was hot and windy in the garden of Our Lady of the Wheat, but inside the convent it was worse. The walls were stifling, the cells infernos, and Isabel had tossed for hours, unable to find a slim thread of forgetfulness. When she finally gave up on sleep, it was almost time for night prayer anyway and so she put on her cotton shift, the flowing brown habit, even her novice's cloak, just in case there should be someone else out walking. Though by night the garden was usually forbidden, this had been such a dry and unforgiving spring that no word of reproach was spoken if a Sister was found at the feet of the Blessed Virgin's shrine asking for her intercession, begging that She save the local farmers by reviving their crops, seeded into dust, the new shoots wilting in the flat alluvial fields.

Just beyond the walls of the convent, the whine and roar of machinery grading the new Interstate by-pass had been constant all month. The swish of air brakes, gears grinding, the unaccustomed shouts of men grated on the women's nerves. Dirt rose, sifted into their linen, feathered over the walls in plumes and spurts. Sand filtered into the rising bread dough, and as the Sisters bit down on tiny particles they closed their eyes and said a quick prayer to keep their tempers.

And yet the presence of the crew was beneficial, useful in some ways. Last week, a representative of the Mother Superior had convinced a couple of workers to lift the statue of Our Lady from Her pedestal and cart Her into town for adoration. Isabel had watched it happen from the small, perfectly square upstairs window of her room. The lineman's crane lowered its gawky arm over the wall, a man got out, three others helped push, pull and wrestle the stone Virgin into the bucket. She rose, Her sheaf of stiff wheat trembling slightly in Her arms. Her face was bare, cool and white. Whatever marble had been used, there were no veins or mars of mineral spots. As She ascended through the dark shrubs, Isabel had noticed that one of the men wore a blue and yellow hat, the same type that her ex-husband, Jack Mauser, used to advertise his construction firm.

Now she knelt at the empty pedestal. Two days ago, she'd also found a memo in her message niche: *Meet me in the garden at midnight.* She rarely checked the box, and the note didn't say

197

which night. Through the long, dark hours, she had argued with herself, and in the garden, each night, she had closed her eyes and tried to restore some continuity to her thoughts. Now, the odour of spent honeysuckle swirled around her shoulders, and grit blew from the path, stinging her cheek.

The wind died down, and Isabel was suddenly alert. From beyond the high board wall—she was sure of it—she heard the drum of a large diesel motor. Now the tyres crunched on the gravel road, and air brakes hissed with a sinking croak.

Though technically a novice, Isabel was tough-minded and experienced, no mere girl just off the farm. She was forty, had two Ph.D.s and an arrest record. She had originally come to this convent to find some escape from herself, some peace, but what had begun as a weekend retreat had lengthened to month after month of quiet living. More than half a year had passed, yet not until the sight of the stained construction hat had Isabel felt true disturbance of her mental repose. With annoyance, she got to her feet, gripped her hands tightly together and stepped away from the statue's base.

Edging into the shadows of the bean vines, Isabel waited.

The motor caught again. She heard the thick whine of the truck's hydraulic lifter, and she looked quickly at the residence to see if any lights went on. The windows glittered, black, sending off reflections of silver-bellied storm clouds. Gibbous, football-shaped, the moon eased out for a moment and suddenly there was enough clear light to see the crane and bucket cresting smoothly over the wall.

The machine hesitated, swaying, and from high in his metal roost Jack Mauser himself gazed down into the garden. He passed over Isabel once, then his eyes returned, and he distinguished her from the pattern of shadows and leaves. He nodded, waved a hand, then pressed the controls and lowered himself. Just above the ground, Mauser stopped the machine and unlatched a small door on the side of the bucket. He was a big man, so he exited sideways, walked over to Isabel. Her silence and lack of surprise seemed to dull his resolution. A cloud flapped across the moon and the wind rushed overhead.

'I came to tell you I'm getting married,' he said.

When she didn't react, he raised his voice. 'You don't know her.'

'Shhhhh.'

Isabel leaned forwards and almost placed her hand on his lips, but the warmth of his breath on her fingers stopped her. Behind the walls, she heard her Sisters stirring in the dark. They owned nothing, not one possession. They rose at this hour to pray for the sins that the rest of the world was busy committing. It was unthinkable that they find Mauser here, and so, to disguise him, Isabel quickly slipped off her cloak and wrapped it around his shoulders, then fastened the catch underneath his chin. Her fingertips brushed the lobe of one ear and he reached towards her, but she ducked away, walked over to the cherry picker, and selected a glowing button marked on the control panel. She pushed the button firmly. Up it floated, disappearing into the night. Brown dirt flew through the air, and she turned to Mauser in its swirl, took his hand. Hearing the back door creak heavily, she pulled him to the base of the statue and shoved him into the niche formed by the pruned boughs of yew and honeysuckle. She tore branches off the bushes and thrust them into his arms.

'Get up there and stand still. Hold these. Put on the hood. Someone's coming.'

When he had done as she asked, Isabel knelt at Mauser's feet and crossed herself.

The air turned blacker, the shadows thickened, the sky rolled in so fast that all the garden trembled. Lightning, caught up in the baskets of the clouds, clenched and unclenched without striking. From the back entry of the convent, now, a tiny stump-like figure tottered, pulling itself along the garden path behind a shining aluminium walker. It was Sister Leopolda, 108 years old, a woman so light and ancient that her bones could barely support the garments of her habit. Though absent-minded, she was still regarded as the next thing to a saint among her Sisters. It was rumoured that she had caused a replication of the marvel of the loaves and the fishes during one lean winter, when a great bowl of custard kept in the convent refrigerator was filled and refilled over the course of many nights.

Louise Erdrich

Leopolda's dreams predicted events, and her advice was often sought, though the meaning of her words had become somewhat obscure. Still, she was venerated, and suffered to make her own rules. Tonight, as she did on many nights, she steered herself to the statue of the Virgin to recite her solitary devotions. But as she drew into the alcove, she saw the edge of Isabel's robe, and stopped.

Isabel pretended to be lost in prayer.

When she spoke, Leopolda's voice was reedy, thin, its tone clear as a flute, perhaps because of her decades of contemplative silence.

'Blessed Mother,' the aged nun addressed the ground. 'Where is my Sister's hand?'

The wind blew Leopolda's outer garment like a balloon and then wrapped it around her body. Isabel leaned over to steady the hunched old woman, whose knees were locked tight. Isabel took each leg in her hands and bent with all her strength, as if the old nun were a large doll.

'Now!' Leopolda's voice rose, breathless and gentle, as Isabel eased her on to the kneeler. The storm had moved closer, up to the walls of the garden. The eye of it appeared to have centred just above the low stone convent, for although the leaves trembled on their stems, the air was almost still.

'Leave me now. Go in peace,' the nun commanded, but Isabel knelt next to her on the edge of an apron of watered lawn that surrounded the shrine, and asked, in a low and respectful voice, if she could join her Sister in her prayers.

'I pray alone,' Leopolda said.

But Isabel could not leave. 'I am only a novice,' she argued, 'but please, let me stay. I can't sleep.'

Though Leopolda's eyes were clouded, her body weak, her strength easily exhausted, there was the danger that in a moment of clarity she might notice Mauser and summon all the others. Or become terrified. Who knew how long it had been since she had seen an unordained man? But although Leopolda was in the habit of absently eating bits of paper or whatever else she found in her fingers when she was hungry, although she gazed for hours at the single rose or zinnia placed next to her bed each morning, although at times she seemed half-way in another world, she was also keen-minded and known for her sudden penetrations of understanding.

'Hear my prayer, hear my prayer, hear my prayer,' Leopolda repeated now, and the firmness in her voice became that of a youthful woman. It was clear to Isabel that Leopolda was beseeching the statue, so she remained kneeling on the scrap of grass, hoping that the nun had forgotten her.

'Tell this one to return to her room,' the nun demanded. 'Go!'

'Sister,' cried Isabel in desperation, 'I need your help.'

'Tomorrow.'

'I won't bother you again. Only tell me,' Isabel thought as quickly as she could, coming up with only a lame miraculous request, ' . . . only tell me what will happen. What does my future hold?'

'That you learn to leave people alone.'

'I'm sorry.' Isabel was stymied. She was at a loss, and finally asked, in spite of Mauser's presence: 'Sister, am I strong enough to endure this life?'

'You don't need strength,' said Leopolda. 'You need manners.'

'I need your wisdom,' Isabel insisted, in complete impatience with the situation. She could feel Mauser enjoying her predicament. 'Before I came here, I lived with a fool.'

'You lived alone?'

From above them, branches rustled.

'No, of course not. I was married. I lived with a man who wanted everything from me, who was absent half the time, who loved other women, who claimed to love me, but allowed terrible things to happen and could never be counted on.'

'Then you may do well here after all. You've had practice.'

'In what?'

'Loving God.'

Isabel was getting nowhere. She was also exhausting Leopolda, and now the old woman seemed to shrink still smaller and to lose some of her vigour. She gave a wisp of a sigh, no more than the shudder of breeze passing through the petals of a flower.

'Oh my beautiful and blessed Sister,' she murmured, 'it is hard to be weak. Hard to be so old. At one time I would have taken up the paddle to the butter churn and given you a whack!' She paused a long while, then continued. 'As long as you insist upon remaining beside me, is there something that you want?'

The sudden kindness in the nun's voice almost shamed Isabel, except that she sensed it was craft, false kindness, a bribe, a ploy to throw her off guard. Nevertheless, she had no choice but to hold her position.

'I beg your indulgence,' Isabel said slowly, and upon hearing a shifting from the figure above her, added with pointed emphasis, 'Sister.'

'You are forgiven, my child,' Leopolda instantly agreed.

'Could you pray alone, then?' Isabel asked. 'As if I wasn't here?'

'You wish to hear my prayer.' The old nun raised her head, though she still was nearly bent in two. 'All right.'

Isabel waited.

'End this torment,' the old nun whispered in a vehement rasp.

Isabel glanced up at Mauser's massive form, and beyond, at the empty garden so immaculately tended.

'Can't you see?' The old nun's voice strengthened. 'Can't you see what love brings? There is no relief to love, no end, no wave, no fall, only a continual ascension.'

'Excuse me?'

The nun waved a crooked hand. 'You asked,' she said. Her fingers were gnarled like the roots of a wormwood bush. She folded back into herself with a high, harsh laugh, the sound of glass scraping glass.

The laugh went on so long that Isabel's blood beat in her ears. It drummed so loudly that she could hear nothing, feel nothing. She found herself breathing jerkily, as though she'd fallen flat and knocked the wind out of herself.

Perhaps she gave some sign of her distress and frustration, or perhaps it was just that the constellation of small events suddenly struck Mauser as ridiculous, too. At any rate, Isabel heard

Mauser laugh. It was a small, private, almost interior laugh. If she hadn't known him intimately for twelve years, she would never have been able to distinguish her former husband's amusement from the wind rattling the grass against the wall. But she did hear it, did know it.

'Will you *shut up*?' she cried.

Silence. The old nun hiccuped. The little sounds she made turned gradually into a laughter so high and penetrating that it almost hurt to listen.

'Hear my prayer! Hear my prayer!' Leopolda mimicked in a light falsetto. 'Help me sleep!' She turned her head to glare at Isabel. 'My story is a tale of burning love, child . . . but you aren't ready.'

'I am!' Isabel leaned closer.

'I wept constantly when I first came down here from my home up north,' the old nun began, her tone suddenly confiding. 'Can you imagine—I was orphaned, with no family but my Sisters, yet I longed for home. I swabbed the swollen throats of Sioux Indians with iodine, sewed up knickers for the cows of devout farmers, wrapped the dead. I prayed by night, I prayed by day. Twice I saw the fields hover in the air like blankets, twice I saw them settle. I've been sick so many times, burned by fire. Diseases, plague, boils. I've eaten what I had to. Fried grubs, gophers, frogs. I taught the settlers to knit, to drink from cups. I prayed by day, I prayed by night.'

Leopolda spoke without inflection, but as she continued on she seemed to bow deeper, drawn towards the earth by gravity, by the weight of her large head, until she tipped too far and her mouth pressed against her chest. Isabel came to her rescue, stretched her outwards like a bow until Leopolda could prop her elbows on the lip of the prie-dieu. With that much clearance, her voice could be clearly heard, and she resumed her story.

'When I was still not much more than a girl, still naïve, I was thrown into a river as a sacrifice by a group of farmers newly arrived from a foreign country. I did not understand their language, and only knew what they were doing, and why, by signs they made. It was a ritual they must have followed during desperate times in the place they came from, and certainly, I do not blame them, for it occurred during a frightful visitation of grasshoppers, when all life went mad. Day after day, the waves, the marching, flying, chewing ocean of these insects overwhelmed us. Dread abounded. Invasions were reported to the east, and some fields had been devoured, but selectively. The ones next to them stood untouched. In this was detected the hand of Satan, or of God.

'It was the confusion in people's minds, between the two, which made such mischief.

'There had been evil rumours that the five of us Sisters, living together in harmony, apart from the town but connected always through the force of prayer, were not as we claimed—servants of Our Lady and Our Lord, but mavens of the devil. Our fields, hand-sown and cultivated, had been spared. That miracle gave these men their bold excuse, and my practice of walking unaccompanied in my prayers, distracted only by God, gave them their opportunity.

'Released, I flew from the men's hands over the river's bank and tumbled, whirling once, twice, in my thick brown garments. How infinitely long that falling seemed to last, how I shook inside, how I feared for myself. Only once before had I been immersed in water, you see, and that had all but ended my life. Then I went under. Even these many years later the moment stands clear. I went down, down to the very bottom, struggling in my gown, my shoes like clods on my feet. I had the sense to tear them off and tried to get my wimple, too, but I had pinned it on tightly that morning. Then there was darkness, and I sank into its murmur. I must have struggled after that, but I do not know how I surfaced; the undertow was a quick dark funnel not visible from the shore. It must have pulled me further downstream, for when I came up, I was alone.

'That is when I had the vision from which I ask now to be released! That's when this started! When I rose to the surface, the world was different. I was afloat, moving grandly down the river—for the current crested near the surface and all I had to do was paddle lightly. Even in my heavy clothes, it took no effort, or very little. My veil floated behind me like a wedding train, and although it could have dragged me under, I was no longer worried. The rush was so swift and strong that I seemed to ride for hours.

' **H**aving drowned—for I drowned in spirit—and revived, I'd lost an old life and gained a new one in which, marvellously, now, I belonged. I had so often been unhappy with things, small grievances against others, penances I imposed upon myself, resentments. I had been lonely. Suddenly, I looked at the banks as they swept by and wondered who could be sad in such a place? *Not I.* All looks different from the middle of a river. In its flow, time is long or infinitesimal, the same. I had new eyes. The astounding branches of the trees that hugged the banks, the hollowed dens of wolves and gophers!

'I lapped the water, took it into me, dirt-green and fresh. I smelled the clean, diving fish. Each scale perfect! I heard the falls. Oh yes, I took the roar that widened before me to be the mouth of a great white drop, and yet I stayed quite calm—though of course I couldn't swim. I moved on faster, faster. But it was not tangled white foam rapids that confronted me, but rather the very cause of my predicament.

'Grasshoppers. I had come to a crossing in their march which will tell you something of their incredible numbers. They had made a floating bridge of themselves, which they constantly repaired by trampling down their brothers and sisters. It was so solid that I stepped on to it like a raft, walked across to the bank, jumped off there on to dry ground.

'Once my feet touched solid earth a fear came over me, a weakness that drained my strength so suddenly that I sank upon the ground and knew nothing more.

'I awoke later, who knows how much later. It was night. I distinguished lamplight, a glowing glass, a roof over me, four walls. I was lying on a bed, covered with a quilt and a sheepskin. The air was heavy and delicious with the smell of cooking venison and I was hungry beyond all measure, for I was young, and never full. A bowl was held to my lips and I moved towards it, lured like an animal. Then I saw the hands that held the bowl, his strong arms, his shoulders, his broad and open face.

'Instantly, I remembered the river, the men who tossed me into it, the long thrilling ride.

'"Who are you?" I asked, but without waiting for an answer I grabbed the bowl and drank its contents with such a steady greed that it was only when I'd reached the very bottom that I realized several things all at once: I was alone in the house; no woman had prepared the soup; and I was naked.

'The sheepskin dropped away from my body, and I felt the slight breeze of his breath along my throat. I had not been naked since I was born, for we young Catholic girls were taught never to change all of our clothes at once, but always to keep some form of covering upon our bodies, even when bathing. It was so new an experience that I thrilled to the scrape of sheer air against me, the tension of fleece and tanned skin. I could not give words to the feeling that crept over me, the warmth along my thighs, the hovering elation, the bands of rippling lightness that engulfed me when he moved closer. I felt him, his hand, brutalized and heavy from work, but gentle as he held my arm and took away the empty bowl, the horn spoon, and wiped my lips. I felt his rough hair as he leaned closer, as he moved his length alongside me on the creaking boards, as he slowly turned me towards him. His breathing deepened, he relaxed, and I lay there, too, spent and comfortable, curled against a sweetly sleeping man, a very tired man who smelled of resin from the wood he'd chopped, of metal from the tools he'd used, of hay, of sweat, of great and nameless things that had never been described to me.

'I lay my head beside him, and although I remained awake for many hours in that beautiful stillness, listening to his even breath, eventually I, too, fell asleep.

'Morning dawned with rain on the wind, the sky a sheet of grey light. I remembered where I was, turned, and found that he was gone. Not only that, but I was lying in no comfortable settler's shack, but in an empty shell of a long-abandoned hovel with the wind whipping through, swallows' nests in the eaves, no sign of the man, no bowl, no track, no spoon, no sheepskin covering or blanket, only my clothes tossed on to me, dry, still smelling of the river, but clean and brushed with his warm hands. I stood in the doorway for a long while, and as I stood there I gradually came to understand what had happened.

'*Through You, with You, in You.* Aren't those beautiful words? For of course I knew my husband long before I met Him, long before He rescued me, long before He fed me broth and held me close to Him all through that quiet night.

'Since then, through the years, my love and wonder have steadily increased. Having met Him just that once, having known Him in a man's body, how could I not love him until death? My affection has grown, deepened, until I felt, many years ago, that I'd attained the highest bliss that it was possible to endure. But that pleasure has continued, and continued. The pain of the body, aching bones, any difficulty, all are as nothing before the cast of sunlight on the kitchen tiles, the singing of my Sisters, the blossoming of my sweet honeysuckle, or the memory of His arms. You know how my dear flowers transport me, each petal. I ask you, how can I bear this miracle a moment longer?'

Leopolda's voice shook with emotion, broke from her like strings ripping from a harp.

'Grant my wish, Tower of Ivory, House of Gold! Consummate this pleasure. Let it be done!'

Confused and at a loss, Isabel had buried her head in her hands, and so she did not witness the struggle Leopolda now undertook. With a terrible effort, as if a tree tried to straighten its own crooked limb, the old nun cocked her head and rolled her eyes upwards, strained impossibly, just a bit more, a little farther, to catch a glimpse of the blessed statue. What she saw transfixed her. Just at the moment that Leopolda managed to locate the icon in her narrow view, it seemed to her that the Virgin leaned down off her pedestal, and ever so gently, as Leopolda stretched out her fingers, transferred the carved bundle she carried into the cradle of the nun's arms.

Leopolda's head snapped back to her chest. Clasping the living leaves to herself, burying her face within the boughs, she was overcome with surpassing peace. It was not even the dry wheat by which we live, not grain that the patroness transformed, but the branches of sweet honeysuckle, which blooms so suddenly and with such intoxicating scent. Leopolda sank down breathing the fragrance of the limp, white petals with such strong and vigorous ecstasy that her heart cracked, she pitched straight over, and was granted her request.

When the nun's body fell with a soft thud, her walker ringing on the stone tiles, Isabel tumbled forwards to try and catch her, and Mauser jumped off his perch. Isabel bent beside the old woman, checked her pulse and found it still, but could not absorb the event and continued to pat her tiny wrist and call her name gently, as if to awaken her. It was not until Mauser put his hands on Isabel's shoulders that Isabel was released from the spell of the tale.

'You killed her,' she said wildly, pushing Mauser's hands away.

He stood shifting his feet while Isabel stared at Leopolda's body. Then abruptly, she got up and began to walk, staggering a bit, until she found her balance and direction and made her way past him towards the back door of the convent. Mauser followed, ready to deny all blame. But Isabel passed through the entrance without looking back, and was gone, leaving him outside the building, beside the wall of mortared fieldstone, too high to climb over. The only exit was through the building. He shook his head, drew the cloak more tightly around his shoulders, then opened the door.

Inside, the convent was a surprisingly ordinary place, not that Mauser had been thinking or expecting much of anything else. Just not this. The hallway was floored with a durable but inexpensive linoleum, and the walls were sheet rock, painted in neutral tones. Dim lights drew him towards the kitchen, which was large and airy, filled with storage cupboards. He hoped he would find an exit, but instead arrived at the foot of a set of stairs. He climbed—it was from the stairwell that he heard the distant rise and fall of the voices of nuns at prayer—and reached the second floor with its long, narrow hall of sleeping cells.

Once he found himself in the nun's most private quarters, Mauser knew that he had to talk to Isabel. He needed something from her, some blessing, so he began to look. He assumed he would locate Isabel's rooms by her familiar objects, her tapestries and antique silver atomizers and African carvings, and he entered four nearly bare cells before he stopped to think.

Each cubicle, a simple rectangle with a slanted roof and one small window, held a cot, a small table with a single drawer, and a built-in cabinet. A crucifix hung on the wall and the only light fixture was a bare bulb. The sameness of the four rooms dizzied Mauser. His vision narrowed.

What could he do? How? He rubbed his chin. The cloak. He crushed it to his face and inhaled lengthily and critically. Then he took it away. He tilted his head backwards, considered, touched his nose to the weave again. Her odour had surely permeated the lanolined fibres, the heavy ink of simple dyes, the cloak itself. Not soap. Not any kind of perfume, of course. Just Isabel. He retrieved a time they had been camping together and he smelled only her—but no, that was smoke of birch caught in her hair. He had it, then, he had it perfectly. The first time he'd kissed her, tasted her. She smelled like . . . apple skins. Not the sweet flesh, but green skins, waxy, tart, before you peel them. He started over, now, began with the first room, crept in and then, cautiously, with a delicate excitement, moved to each nun's bed, drew the cover down, and took a breath of the air above the sheet.

He smelled the bottom of a cup of milk in one room, sulphur in the next, he smelled pockets of simmering minerals deep in the earth. He smelled blood, salt, oats and fresh nails, straight from the hardware hopper. Dough, risen but left too long beneath the towel. He smelled apricots, rough cedar and moth-balls. Wool, and that peculiar sharp dry odour that rises when it is pressed. He smelled young hair and old hair. And finally he came to Isabel.

The actual smell of her hit him with a shock that made his mouth water. He smoothed the coverlet back on to her bed, and sat down to wait.

The exhaustion of the past week caught up with Isabel and she almost fell asleep during prayer. She had run into the convent thinking to fetch help, but once there, an overwhelming, numb lassitude had overtaken her. Sleep fizzed in her brain, her face seemed to hum with the solid weight of slumber, and she couldn't open her mouth, didn't know what to say at all. So she told herself that in the light of her own tale, Leopolda wouldn't mind lying in the grass until she was naturally discovered, that it would do no good, anyway, to cause an uproar. Let her rest in peace with her flowers, thought Isabel as her eyes drooped shut. That was the thing to do.

When prayer was over, Isabel made her way down the hall almost sleep-walking. Leopolda's voice still turned in her mind, and the wind rising outside the walls sounded like the rushing of that powerful river that had swept the nun into the arms of her saviour. Isabel lifted the latch on her door, and closed it behind her as she snapped on the light.

Mauser sat on the bed, her cloak neatly folded beside him. His hands rested in his lap, rough and calm. He raised a finger and pointed at the unshaded bulb. Isabel put her palm down on the switch and the room went dark.

Her head cleared immediately. She felt the old anger whirr along her spine.

'Get out of here, Jack.'

Mauser had a large frame, muscular and heavy, the build of an older football star, though his wrists and ankles were elegant and narrow. When he slumped, as he did now, overcome suddenly with the physical weight of his own body, he lost some of his grace, and that made him look affectingly young. Even in the dark, Isabel could sense the way he shifted into uncertainty.

'I'm sorry . . . ' His voice was shamed and quiet.

'She was over a hundred years old.'

Mauser didn't move, didn't speak again. Isabel touched his hand.

'It's just that I, you know, it was like she asked me when she stuck out her arms, like she wanted the flowers. I wouldn't have done it otherwise. I wouldn't have even thought of it.'

'Well she probably . . . I don't know.'

'Should we go and get her?'

'No.'

Lightning rattled in the eaves, and Mauser and Isabel watched each other in its glare. The wind had slammed the casement shut. Isabel walked over and jerked open the window. Fresh air poured in, cooler, stiffened at its edges by that before-rain fragrance of stirred dust. They were silent for a long while before Isabel spoke.

'So. Wife number five,' she said. 'When's the happy day?'

'Tomorrow.'

Just as Isabel laughed, a jagged branch of lightning whipped the ground, miles off, and they heard the thunder bound towards them. One second. Two. Three. Then the noise closed with a dense, emphatic, comforting solidity, as if a child's hollow block had been clapped over the convent.

'Oh, the hell with you.' Isabel struggled out of her over-garment, threw it down at her feet, and stood before Mauser. 'No one's going to hear us, so we might as well talk.'

She was wearing a rough shift, and as they sat together Mauser took the cloth absently between his fingers and rubbed it.

'Cotton,' she said before he asked.

He nodded, and dropped the fold of material. Isabel's hair was short, thick with the stormy air's watery electricity. She pushed Mauser back on the bed, reached into the crack of her bedside drawer and took out a thin roll of toilet-paper. Within it, a single cigarette was hidden, along with a kitchen match. She lit the cigarette, inhaled deeply, passed it sideways.

'So. What's she like?'

Mauser drew and offered the cigarette back to her. He spoke normally, his voice obscured by the restless night. He sounded like himself again, intimate and half-drunk with eagerness, as he poured out the story. She was younger, and a bit, well, strong-minded. Tough. Isabel would like her, though she was almost boyish. She had a daughter, twelve years old. She was not a brain, like Isabel, but she was smart. He was giving her books. She loved Mauser, that was in her favour, wasn't it? He told his first wife all he could, every detail he could think of, and then he reclined against the wall, his limbs relaxed and sprawling, his legs long and heavy.

'You're not going to fall asleep on me here.'

'No . . . ' He waited, his breathing shallow, refusing to let her off the hook.

Louise Erdrich

'I hope you two are happy,' Isabel said, finally, in a light, flat voice.

Brightness froze the air in the room. The sound was simultaneous with the long pulse of radiance and the singe of ozone filled their lungs. Mauser's face appeared again before Isabel—big, handsome, the mouth a little petulant, the eyes ice-blue and Slavic. Isabel reclined carefully against him on the narrow cot.

'Forget it, Jack,' she warned when he began to trace her chin and throat with his fingers.

He dropped his hand and held her around the waist and the two drowsed as the rain splashed against the window, quietly, just a few drops. Then it diminished to nothing. As the intensity of the weather passed into the distance, it was as though something huge was walking away, across the plains. Isabel's last thought before sleep was a wish. If she could get up and push through the wall into the field, if she could follow the thunder, she could get where she wanted to go.

From the night of Jack Mauser's visitation, Isabel began to lose sleep. Lightning had evidently struck the cherry picker, as it stayed poised at its highest reach, just beyond the wall. Instead of grounding harmlessly, the spark leaped, surged towards something in the garden path, probably Sister Leopolda's shiny walker, which was found later—twisted, blackened, and somehow shrunk no larger than a pair of bobby pins. Leopolda herself lay next to it, a pile of ash in the shape of a cross. Of course, there were those who saw a new miracle in this, and there was even talk of fixing the holy ash in place and putting the whole site under glass, consecrating it as a shrine. But before the Bishop could be summoned and matters arranged, a strong, fresh wind arose and blew the powder that had been Leopolda straight into the honeysuckle bushes, where she mingled with pollen.

Pausing at the still-empty base of the statue that morning, Isabel watched as the dust of the holy woman was carried off by bees. Of course, it was probably what she would have wanted, just like her to be transported on the feet of insects, turned to

212

honey. But perhaps because Isabel had torn off the bough for Mauser and now remembered that its bloom was over, its season finished, she was the only one who paid attention to the fact that for three new weeks the blossoms on the honeysuckle bushes renewed in such dense profusion and number that the fragrance wafted half-way around the building at night and through her window, waking her with its insistent sweetness, loosening her limbs beneath the blanket, causing her to lie suspended in the darkness, filling her head with such thoughts.

Mauser's visit had upset her. Now that he had invaded her room, she found herself thinking of him again, and once her inward vision turned upon him she could not relinquish vivid pictures in spite of everything she tried. Prayers were useless—too passionate—and reminded her that what she had felt for Mauser at its best was a desperate kind of love, which had turned into its own opposite. Still, she could not help but dwell on its deepest moments. She wished she hadn't knocked his hand away on that stormy night, either, and she kept waiting for the long continuation of his gesture.

Just one night, she kept thinking, just that one night would have been enough. Then I could have returned, contented, to this orderly and satisfying life.

But her peace was shattered, as if the storm had blasted everything. After several weeks, during which her temptation did not abate, Isabel knew that the awful and unpredictable thing, which had happened several times during their marriage, was happening to her once again. She was falling in love with her own husband. He wouldn't leave her mind. His image drenched her. The turn of his wrist, the weave of expressions on his face, the clothes he had worn the last time she saw him, all of these things became the articles of faith in the house constructed of her wakefulness. She began to wish she'd made Mauser leave something behind, something, a souvenir, anything. She wanted his clothing. She wanted his ice-blue shirt. His slacks, which were made of a material rough and tan. She wanted things he'd worn when they were married. His work jacket came back to her, heavy with male significance. She saw it, polished on the cuffs with grease and oiled on the back where Mauser slid underneath

his car. She wanted the pockets—his hands had stuffed into
them, loose fists—and she wanted the collar that had touched his
neck.

After a month, two months of this, sleep entirely evaded
her. She began to dread entering her room, and hated the
bed itself, its flat pillow and mattress filled with
buckwheat hulls. She lay on the floor some nights, curled up in
the corner, and drifted. By day she started to unravel. She could
feel her nerves, the fibres splitting, twanging off like bow-strings.
She could feel her head enlarging. It was stuffed with soft lumps
of cotton wadding. She could feel it up there, above her eyes,
porous, absorbing her experience. She had always feared going
without sleep, and now she was hostage to its loss. She could get
no medicine, of course, and was only allowed one book in her
room besides the New Testament.

What would she have picked a year ago, she wondered, to
bring to her desert island of a room? Perhaps a VCR and the
collection of Madonna's videos, or the journals of Princess
Labanne DeBoer. Now, those things made her shudder. She
wanted dry matter, the driest she could find. There was very little
to choose from in the convent library, but at least it was all
harmless stuff, and she did have a favourite, which she took out
time after time and lugged to her nightstand. *The New York
Public Library Desk Reference* became her only reading, for
weeks. When desperate, she opened it at random, memorized
pure information, as if she could block out Mauser with facts and
statistics. She knew the foreign currencies of every country in the
world, knew by heart all of the visa requirements, and became an
expert on stain removal. Fish slime? Lukewarm solution of salt
water. Correction fluid? Amyl acetate. Chewing gum? Freeze it.
But she never stained her clothes at the convent, nothing clung to
her, not even the juice of the grapes she squeezed through a
cheesecloth to make jelly, not even ink. It was when she had
finally used up another month of nights mastering the tables of
the nutritive values of food—when she said grace one morning
over her soft-boiled egg and thought *73.3% water, 12.7 grams of
protein, 11.6 of fat, 0 fibre content, 1.4 grams of ash*, and on,

down to the last contained milligram of ascorbic acid—that Isabel began to accept that she was in trouble.

There was 'ash' in almost every food, but was it really *ash*, like wood ash, the ash of things burnt way back from the beginning of time, including Sister Leopolda? Isabel's sense of taste became so keen that she could actually taste in each mouthful the haunted image of things that had burned—the spines and floors of houses, piles of yellow leaves, trash of sugar beets, people, dogs, cows, cats, all kinds of trees, hills of straw, newspapers, bags, random garbage. Most days she hardly took two bites. The food crumbled on her lips. The most innocuous substances—oatmeal, almonds—turned on her tongue. She could not untie her throat to swallow, could not breathe except from the livid space around her heart. She trembled at the shutting of a door, and strange notions came into her head.

Cut your own throat, now. She kept hearing that odd line from the Robert Lowell poem as she worked with knives in the kitchen. Outside, labouring on the convent grounds, she found good resolutions, but also discovered herself hoping that a tree would fall, a snapped limb pierce her dead. Streams of wild energy flowed through her arms and legs, and one night she washed every already clean dish in the convent house, scrubbed every floor and hall the next.

'This,' approved the Mother Superior, 'is a sign of the profound love you bear. You are close.'

Nearer, nearer.

Isabel had subsisted for one week like Saint Theresa, on nothing more than distilled water and communion wafers, when she collapsed. She was immediately taken to the small hospital in the town near the convent, where, because no private rooms were available, she took a bed in the ward. There, surrounded by only two layers of tan drapes, in a noisy barracks of women recovering from various ills and surgeries, Isabel at least could sleep.

In fact, she slept so profoundly, for almost a solid week, that the doctors came in periodically to check for certain that she had not slipped into a coma. But it was genuine sleep, the purest rest she'd had since childhood. The sound of talking soothed her, the

clank of bedpans calmed her, the groans of other woman in the
dead of night lulled her into a deeper plateau of unconsciousness.
When she woke, she swallowed the warm jello waiting on her
tray. When she lay back, sleep stole immediately over her again,
a warm blanket, smothering all thoughts.

In the end, the summer gone to heat and loneliness and
sexual strain, the short growing season nearly finished, Isabel
simply rose, walked out of the ward and down a corridor where
she used the patients' lounge telephone. She called Jack Mauser,
who wasn't home, but in his absence she struck up an
uncomfortable conversation with his new wife, Dot, who
expressed concern over Isabel's plight and promised that she
would tell Jack where Isabel was as soon as he came home. A
couple of days went by. Perhaps Jack hadn't received the message
after all, Isabel thought, or perhaps the bitch never said a word.
She tried to control her thoughts, dialled and redialled his office
number until finally she got Mauser on the line.

'Jack.'

'What's up?'

'I'm in the hospital. I was sick, but I'm well now. I need
someone to get me.'

'Sure.'

His voice was so calm and full and deep that the place
around her heart pulsed suddenly, as though a match were set to
alcohol.

'Anything you want me to bring?'

'Stop at the liquor store,' she managed to say. 'Buy me a
good Cabernet. I'll pay you back.'

'Anything else?'

'A sandwich,' Isabel's mouth filled suddenly, her eyes. 'Oh
God. Black pastrami, dark rye, hot mustard, and a kosher
pickle.'

'I f you'd only said something, Jack,' Dot sounded more hurt
than angry, at least at first, and that made Mauser wary.
She was being too nice. Her voice was merely thick and
puzzled. 'When she called me I was floored. I didn't know what
to say. You never told me, Jack. Didn't you trust me?'

'I do trust you.'

'Well then, tell me.' Dot's voice jumped higher, shook with loose gravel. 'What kind of man has a former wife who goes off to be a nun in a convent and has a nervous breakdown? What kind of man keeps in touch with her, takes her phone calls, bails her out?'

Mauser was almost reassured by the quick attack, hoping that would be the worst she did. He opened his mouth, but before the words came out, Dot answered herself.

'You do nice things for other people. I know that. You pay their bar tabs. You give big gifts. You built me a bookshelf out of rock maple, and I only have a couple books. You carved my daughter a mask. Now you're making her a tennis racket. God knows what you made for this crazy wife you had. You can't keep track and you won't give anything up. At least my husband, my former husband, is in jail for life. He can't bother you, call you. You don't know what it's like, how threatening an ex can be.'

'Don't be threatened,' said Mauser. 'Come here.'

Dot stood where she was, staring in a blind heat. She was big, red-haired, self-conscious, thirty-five, with hair sprayed carefully to look both wild and free. She outlined her dark eyes with exotic-looking eyeliner. Her lips were red, her chin stubborn. Mauser went to her. She stood stiff as a post. He stepped closer and put his arms around her.

'Don't be threatened,' he repeated, in a gentler tone. 'You can even come along. Would that make you happy?'

'Happy? Not exactly, no.'

Mauser kept holding her until she shrugged him off.

'What can I do? Tell me. In your mind, what can I do?'

Dot hugged herself and looked at the ground. She ran her hands up and down the buttons of her shirt.

'Oh,' she whispered at last, 'I don't know.'

They took the old highway out of Fargo instead of the Interstate. It was a beautiful road and even had some long swelling curves in it, fun to drive. The wheat had been harvested that week and the stubble glowed. Tall white egrets paced along the far edges, a blue heron or two; blackbirds gathering to migrate exploded upwards in great sudden disintegrating spirals, their pattern shattering and swirling in the clear air. About half-way to Argus a lark flew at them, flashed yellow, disappeared. Mauser started, slowed, looked into the rear-view mirror, then settled back.

'I think I missed it,' he smiled at his wife.

Dot looked at him. Her gradient sixties-style sun-glasses made her face remote and tough. 'Tell me one thing,' she said. 'Was it better, I mean, with her?'

'Oh for Christsakes, Dot, what do you want me to say?'

Dot picked up a pair of knitting needles and began jabbing them in and out of a pastel froth of yarn. She cleared her throat impatiently a couple of times and then threw the project to the floor of the car.

'No,' she said. 'I want you to say to me, "no".'

'No,' said Mauser.

'Thank you. Thank you very much.'

The hospital was made of brown bricks, with white gables and wooden porches, and the large lot overlooked a swift-flowing, narrow brown river. Jack parked carefully, and they both got out. Dot stretched her arms over her head and swung her hips back and forth. Jack went around the front to check the grille.

'Hell, I did get it,' he said after a moment.

The meadowlark was tucked where the bumper met the curve of red metal. There was no visible damage—in fact the small bird looked natural and comfortable, as though perched asleep, its wings folded flat along the black V, along the yellow of its breast.

'You sure did.' Dot scooped the bird from the car in one quick motion, carried it over to the trash can by the sidewalk, and tossed it in.

'Hey,' Mauser called to his wife. 'You can't just throw a bird away like that.'

'Hey, you're the one who hit it.'

Mauser glanced around uncertainly as they walked towards

the hospital. The ground was tarred, with carefully painted white lines. The sidewalks were bounded by thick mats of clipped brown grass. There was nowhere, actually, to put a bird, no turned earth—not that he'd want to bury it, but the thing was, he didn't know exactly what he should have done. As they walked through the clear double doors of the place, Mauser took shallow breaths of stale white hospital air. Even the elevator smelled of medicines.

'One thing I don't want to do,' he told Dot suddenly, thinking of it for the first time as the elevator doors squeezed shut and they ascended. 'I don't want to die in a hospital.'

She looked at him assessingly. 'Who does?'

'I mean it. I'd rather die anywhere else than in a hospital.'

'OK,' said Dot. 'You got it. Now let's pick up the fruit-cake and bring her home.'

Once on the ward, they walked to the desk and Mauser identified himself. The nurse regarded them searchingly.

'Will Mrs Mauser be leaving us, then?'

'Yes,' said Jack. 'We're driving her back to Fargo.'

The woman's expression lightened, and she lifted a stack of papers into her arms. 'Follow me.'

'She's so glad, I can tell,' Dot whispered to her husband. 'That poor gal is ready to ditch your Isabel.'

'Here she is!' With a flourish, the nurse swept away the curtains that hung around the hospital bed. Upon it, straight-legged on the smooth coverlet, her back propped on pillows and a pile of books beside her, was Isabel. She had lost weight. Her face was gaunt, the stern lines deeper carved. Her thick grey-black Black German hair curved off her forehead and her eyes burned deep in the sockets.

'God, am I ever glad to see you,' she said to Mauser. 'Hi,' she nodded to Dot.

'Hi,' Dot answered automatically. Isabel hardly looked like a rival. In spite of her fierce glare at the nurse, she seemed pitiful. Her thinness was almost shocking, and made her teeth stand out; the expression in her great dark eyes was so penetrating that Dot nearly lost composure. She almost shuddered when Jack offered

Isabel the sandwich and she snatched at it with greedy claws.

'Let me help you. Here.' Dot moved to her side. She gestured at the nurse. 'A wheelchair?'

And so, with Dot leading them through the process, prompting, pushing, they made their way from the hospital. Mauser manoeuvred the car to the door, and Dot helped settle Isabel into the back seat. She propped the half-knit afghan beneath one of Isabel's arms, and leaned across to buckle her seat-belt.

'You're kind to take the trouble.' Isabel looked into Dot's face. 'How do you get your liner on so smoothly? It's perfect.'

Dot felt Isabel's breath on her neck. She paused, their faces only inches apart.

'I use a little paintbrush.' Dot's voice choked in her throat. Isabel blinked curiously at her, and Dot walked around to get in the front seat beside Mauser.

'She's wonderful,' Isabel was saying as Dot settled herself. 'You're very lucky, Jack, I hope you know that. I hope you're taking good care of her, not just in material ways, either. It's clear you made the right choice; I can't tell you how I worried. Congratulations.'

'You worried?' Dot looked back over her shoulder as they pulled out of the lot.

Isabel frowned slightly, nodded, met her eyes in guileless complicity.

'Of course I did. After Chetta? Or don't you know about Chetta. Jack?'

'Who's Chetta?' Dot leaned across the seat, her profile keen and motionless as a bird dog's. 'What's she talking about?'

Jack reached over as if to turn on the air conditioning, but then put his hand back on the wheel with a decisive motion.

'I was going to tell you, at the right time. See, there was another wife.'

'What do you mean?' Dot spoke slowly, almost stupidly, leaning back into the web of her seat-belt. 'Before Isabel?'

'No. After. Between her and you. It was very short.'

'You bastard.'

Isabel put her hands in her lap, and tried to look out the

window without glancing towards the rear-view mirror, which, she knew, held Mauser's glare.

'I shouldn't have said anything.'

'Shut up, Isabel,' said Mauser.

But Isabel continued as soon as they were on the highway. 'Jack met her at a time when he wasn't thinking with a clear mind. Of course,' she added, after a pause, speaking over Dot's shoulder, 'Jack was thinking very, very clearly when he met you, I'm sure.'

'Fuck you,' said Dot. 'And you call yourself a nun.'

'You might as well get it done with,' Jack spoke loudly, desperately, taking both hands off the wheel. He rammed them back again before the car veered into the ditch. 'Tell her everything you know about me. Wreck this one too, Isabel. Why not? You did a tap-dance on the others.'

'Others?'

Dot swivelled to the back seat, her face hard and tight beneath her even tan, her dark eyes sharp as darts. 'Since he won't tell me, you tell me. Tell me about the others.'

'I'll tell you. What do you want to know?' said Mauser.

'How many, first of all.'

'Five.' He spoke quickly, before Isabel could answer. 'Five, counting you.'

'Five? I'm the goddamn *fifth*?'

Dot tossed her head to the side, as if she had been slapped, then hunched over, seemed to gather herself in, but suddenly exploded in motion. She jabbed her arms down near her legs into the foamy yarn of her knitting bag and pulled out a thin blue metal needle. Mauser saw the flash of it in her hands and ducked forwards, wrenching the wheel just as Dot plunged at him, grazing his neck, sinking the needle deeply into the back cushion of his seat. She unfastened herself and began to rummage in the yarn again.

'Jesus!' Mauser cried. 'Stop her!'

Isabel lunged over the back seat and tried to buckle herself around Dot, but Dot easily unlatched her pinched arms. Mauser stopped the car in the breakdown lane, and grabbed for Dot's wrists.

'Calm down,' he said. 'Get a hold of yourself. I was going to tell you—honestly—but I was scared you'd react this way.'

'Scared? You were scared?'

Mauser nodded, held on to her with one hand and lightly stroked her arms with the other. He bent over once and kissed her, carefully, and kept on touching her with soothing grace until the tightness left her face, gradually, and her clenched fingers relaxed. She dropped the second needle, then shrugged from Mauser's grip.

'I'm still the same guy you married,' he said.

'No, you're not.' Dot tore away from him. Her voice was tired. 'I don't know you from shit.' She turned away from him and looked out the side window, resting her head against the back of her seat.

No one said anything for a long time after that, and then, finally, Mauser started the car and pulled out on to the road. He began to go faster, faster, up to the speed limit, then past it. The seams in the concrete road struck the wheels hard and fast. On either side, fields of ripening sunflowers, their heads black and drooping, turned like chains, blurring into the dusk.

'Well, you know what I always say,' Mauser said at last, his voice ripping the hum of the air pocket the car moved within.

Nobody asked what he always said, so he shouted.

'I say something simple-minded like, "let's listen to a little music."' He slammed a tape into the slot above the radio and Sam Cook's voice looped slowly, hoarsely, on the highest volume. *Well I'm staring at the wishing well.*

It was not for quite a while, not until the tape came to an end, in fact, and Mauser slowed down and quieted himself and reached to the machine, that he noticed, in the interval before the second side began, that both women were weeping steadily and wrenchingly, behind him, beside him, in his own throat, with the same unceasing rhythm and regularity as the cracks of pavement against the wheels.

ADAM MARS-JONES
BEARS IN MOURNING

When I think about it, it was terrible the way we behaved when Victor died. We behaved as if we were ashamed of him, or angry. It didn't show us at our best—we didn't cope at all well. We all knew Victor was 'ill', obviously, but none of us really took on board how bad things had got.

He was in the middle of our little group, our sect, but somehow he got lost all the same. I suppose each of us paid him some token attention—his conversation tended to go round in circles, particularly with the drink—and then left it to somebody else to do the real work: supporting him and talking him through the dark days. He was our brother Bear, but the fraternity didn't do well by him.

We Bears are a varied crowd. There's an organist, a social worker, a travel agent, an osteopath. That's not the full list, of course, that's off the top of my head. If it wasn't for membership of the Bear nation we would have nothing in common. Somehow we always thought that would be enough.

It's amazing that Victor was able to hold down his job for as long as he did, but then he'd done it for a long time. He was working with friends, people who would make allowances. In any case there was a structure set up, and within limits it ran itself. Every few months Victor, or rather the company that employed him, put out the first issue of a magazine devoted to some sure-fire subject—French cookery, classic cars, sixties pop. When I say the first issue, I mean of course Parts One and Two, Part Two coming free.

It doesn't take long, with a half-way decent picture researcher, to get enough stuff from reference books to fill a few magazine pages. Tasters for future issues take care of the rest. Part Three never arrives, and maybe people wonder why not. Maybe they think, shame nobody bought Parts One and Two—it was such a good idea. Pity it didn't catch on.

I used to wonder what would have happened if one of Victor's magazines had really taken off, had sold and sold off the news-stands. Would there have come a time when Part Three became inevitable? I don't think so. I think Victor's employers would have carried on repackaging their little stack of ideas for ever. With a little redesign, they could put out the same Parts

One and Two every two years or so. Which they did.

Victor was prime Bear, Bear absolute. I know I haven't explained just what a Bear is, and it's not an easy thing to define. There have always been tubby men, but I can't think they ever formed a little self-conscious tribe before. *Tubby* isn't even the right word, but at least it's better than *chubby*. *Chubby* is hopeless, and *chubby-chaser* is a joke category.

To be a Bear you need, let's see, two essential characteristics, a beard and a bit of flesh to spare, preferably some body hair. But it's a more mysterious business than that. Some men will never be Bears however hairy they are, however much surplus weight they carry. They just look like hairy thin guys who've let themselves run to seed, thin men who could stand to lose a few pounds. A true Bear has a wholeness you can't miss—at least if you're looking for it.

It's a great thing to watch a Bear become aware of himself. All his life he's been made to feel like a lump, and then he meets a person, and then a whole group, that thinks he's heaven on legs. On tree-trunk legs. He's been struggling all his life against his body, and suddenly it's perfect. There have been quite a few lapsed health-club memberships in our little circle, I can tell you.

One of them was mine. I remember the first time I was hugged by a Bear, as a Bear. We were Bear to Bear. I remember how his hand squeezed my tummy—*tummy*'s a childish word but the others are worse—and I realized I didn't need to hold it in. He wasn't looking for a wash-board stomach, the sort you can see in the magazines. He was happy with a wash-tub stomach like mine. He liked me just the way I was.

And Aids, Aids. Where does Aids come into this?

All of us were involved in the epidemic in some way, socially, politically, rattling collection buckets at benefit shows if nothing else. And of course we were all terrified of getting sick. But that's not what I'm getting at.

Aids is like the weather. It doesn't cause everything, but the things it doesn't cause it causes the causes of. So, yes, you'd think there'd be a link between a group of men who like their lovers to have a bit of meat on their bones, who like men with curves, and a disease that makes people shrivel away into a straight line up and down.

But I don't really think so. The Bear idea would have happened with or without Aids. The English language had a hand in it, by putting the words *bear* and *beard* so close to each other in the dictionary. Perhaps it's a sexual style that works differently in other languages. Has anyone in history ever really enjoyed beards, let alone based a little erotic religion around them? I suppose Victorian wives were the people in history most exposed to facial hair, and they weren't in much of a position to shop around or compare notes.

The beard is a mystery worn on the face. There are beards of silk and beards of wire, each with its charge of static, and it isn't easy to tell them apart without a nuzzle, or at least a touch of the hand.

We in our group are great observers of the way a beard shows up different pigments from the rest of the head hair. Ginger tints are common; less often, we see magical combinations of darkness and blondness. Beards age unpredictably, sometimes greying before the head hair, sometimes retaining a strong shade when all colour has drained from the scalp. The first frost may appear evenly across the beard, or locally in the sideboards, or on the chin, or at the corners of the mouth.

We in our group are tolerant of tufty beards, wispy beards, beards with asymmetrical holes. There are beards that Nature more or less insists on, to cover up her botches. Only a few bearers of the beard, we feel, positively bring it into disrepute, usually by reason of fancy razorwork. The beard to us is more than a sexual trigger, not far short of a sexual organ. Some of us even defend jazzman beards, goatees, beards that look like a few eyebrows stuck together. As a group, we particularly admire a beard that rides high on the cheeks, or one that runs down the neck unshaven.

Bears don't discriminate against age. It's just the other way about. We often say that someone is too young for his beard—he'll have to grow into it.

A man with a pure-white beard can expect as many looks of appreciation, still tinged with lust, as someone twenty, thirty years younger. There are many couples in our group, though few

227

of them even try to be monogamous, and some of them are made up of figures who we might describe as Bear and Cub, Daddy Bear and Baby Bear—but even they don't take their roles very seriously. Neither of them tries too hard to play the grown-up.

It's as if in every generation of boy children there are a few who put their fingers in their ears during tellings of *Goldilocks*, filtering out the female elements in the story, until what they are left with is a fuzzy fable of furry sleepers, of rumpled beds and porridge.

Every happy period is a sort of childhood, and the last ten years have been a happy period for the Bears, in spite of everything.

So when I say that Victor was an absolute Bear, I mean that he had pale skin, heavy eyebrows and a startlingly dark beard, full but trimmed. No human hair is black, even Chinese or Japanese, and Raven Black hair dye is sold as a cruel joke to people who know no better, but Victor's came close. He was forty-two or three then, I suppose, and five foot eight, ideal Bear height. He pointed his feet out a bit, as if his tummy was a new thing and needed a new arrangement of posture to balance it.

We met in a bar. Under artificial light the drama of his colouring wasn't immediately obvious, and I mistook him for a German who had been rude to me in another bar a couple of months before. I suppose my body language expressed a pre-emptive rejection, which in the event Victor found attractive. After a while he came over to me and said, 'You win. You've stared me down. Let me buy you a drink.'

I went home with him in his old Rover to Bromley, an unexpectedly long journey, and a suburban setting that didn't seem to fit with the man who took me there. Later I learned that this had been his childhood home. When his mother died, Victor had let go a West End flat so as to keep his father company. It was a doomed gesture, as things turned out—one of a series —because his father soon found some company of his own. The companion may in fact have dated back to days before Victor's mother died.

It was late when we arrived at Bromley. I assumed we were

alone in the house, in which case Victor's father was stopping out with his lady friend, but perhaps he was asleep in a bedroom I didn't see. If so, he slept soundly, and got up either before or after we did.

The bedroom was in chaos, but not knowing Victor it didn't occur to me to wonder whether it was an ebullient chaos or a despairing one. There was a big bulletin board on the mantelpiece, with photographs, letters and business cards pinned up on it, but there was still an overflow of paper and magazines. There was the inevitable shelf of Paddingtons, Poohs and koalas, and a single Snoopy to show breadth of mind.

Victor wanted first to be hugged and then fucked. He mentioned that this second desire was a rarity with him, and I could believe him. He was vague about the location of condoms. Eventually I found a single protective in a bedside drawer, of an unfamiliar brand (the writing on the packet seemed to be Dutch) and elderly appearance. I could find no lubricant that wouldn't dissolve it. I put it on anyway, to show willing, and lay down on top of Victor. I enjoyed the heat and mass of the man beneath me; I made only the most tentative pelvic movements, just vigorous enough to tear the dry condom. Then Victor remembered that he had some lubricant after all, under the bed.

Victor was apologetic about the confusion of our sexual transaction, but looking back I find it appropriate. He was both in and out of the world, even then, and he could summon up separately the elements of love-making, desire, caution, tenderness, but not string them together.

At some stage I noticed he was crying, and he went on for over an hour before he stopped. I hugged him some more, but I can't say that I took his distress very seriously. I didn't make anything of the fact that we didn't have a particularly good time in bed. Good sex isn't very Bear, somehow. I was already well used to awkwardness, lapses of concentration, sudden emotional outpourings. What could be more Bear than a fatherly man on a crying jag?

Bears are never far from tears, or wild laughter come to that. I have seen Bears cry just as hard as Victor did that night, beards matted with their tears, and be cheered up by a bowl of cereal or a cartoon on television. But of course Victor only stopped crying when he fell asleep. The curtains were open, and it was already beginning to get light. I hate sleeping like that—this Bear likes his cave dark—but I didn't stay awake long enough to do anything about it.

That was my only intimate contact with Victor, but the Bear community continued to revolve in its eccentric orbit around him. Everybody I met seemed to know him, and I ended up keeping track of him without making any great effort. Victor's father died a few months after we met, which I think was the great event in Victor's life. After that he had a succession of room-mates at the house—Bears, inevitably. They didn't stay long. Victor was hard going by then, even for Bears. But while they stayed, and while he stayed coherent, Victor took a fatherly interest in them, and would try to fix them up with compatible Bruins. That's a nice characteristic—that's a good thing to remember.

I invited Victor to dinner once about that time, and he phoned me on the evening arranged to warn me he'd be late. He never arrived. From friends on the Bear grape-vine I learned that this pattern was typical.

After Victor died, the room-mate at the time wanted everything of Victor's, everything that was even reminiscent of Victor, cleared away at once. He wasn't being heartless, he just couldn't cope with a dead man's presence being imprinted so strongly on the rooms. I went along to help out, but it wasn't as straightforward a job as I had thought when we started. Apparently neutral objects kept leaping into hurtful life.

It turned out that Victor used to offer himself as a photographic model for his magazines and their stable-mates. Surprising that a man with low self-esteem should so much enjoy being photographed. But apparently he used to tease the company's photographic editor about the scarcity of bearded images in the media, and offered himself to make good the lack. So as we cleared the room we found that the slippered individual on the cover of a mid-seventies hi-fi magazine, head cocked while he stroked a spaniel and listened to a hulking array of quadrophonic speakers, was a mid-seventies Victor. The genial chef on another cover, stirring a golden sauce in a kitchen hung with gleaming copper pans, was also Victor. Victor was even a tasteful Adam on the cover of a pop-psychology mag, Parts One and Two, receiving a glossy apple from an Eve with scheming eyes. Finally all the traces of Victor's presence were gone, stuffed under beds or bundled into bin-bags.

The worst part of the visit, though, was finding in Victor's waste-paper basket something that was like the opposite of a suicide note. It was the note he would have left for his room-mate if Victor had managed to decide to go on living. *Dear Bear*, it started, and it said

Sorry I've been so hard to be around lately, that's the last thing you need. Thanks for bearing it anyway (bad joke), and I think I've turned the corner. I'll leave the car tomorrow—no point in taking it—and I'll see you in the p.m. Don't chuck the *Guardian*, there may be some jobs in it. Love Victor.

I had known that Victor was due to appear in court the next day for drunk driving (not his first offence) and was certain to lose his licence. I hadn't heard that he had also lost his job, which was probably because of his general unreliability, although the pretext had to do with fiddling expenses or paying somebody who was already on the staff to do piece-work under another name.

Instead of turning up in court, and instead of leaving the note, which he crumpled up and threw in the waste-paper basket, Victor took the car and drove down to the country, Kent somewhere, I'm afraid I've blotted out the details. I think it was where his parents met, or had their first date, or went on their honeymoon. It had a private significance, but I've forgotten exactly what. I imagine it was a beauty spot, and that he reached it in the early hours. He must have waited a bit, after he arrived, for the crumbling exhaust pipe of the old Rover to cool down from the journey. He wouldn't have wanted to burn his hands or melt the hose. Perhaps he waited again afterwards, before he restarted the engine.

He didn't leave a note, but he hardly needed to. For weeks he had been sitting around drinking and listening to a record—the first single he had bought for years, I dare say. It was called *The Living Years* by Mike and the Mechanics, and by bad luck it was at number one. For a few weeks it was impossible to avoid it on the radio. It was all about not telling your father you loved him while he was alive, and Victor played it over and over again. Mike of the Mechanics is one of the very few beards in pop music, but I don't think that had anything to do with it. Far too lanky to be a Bear.

Victor had a little bag of runes, a sort of Celtic *I Ching*, given him by an Irish Bear who used them to make every decision, and he would draw a rune from the bag every now and then when he was drinking. He seemed to draw the blank tile rather a lot, or so I heard, from the black suede draw-string bag. The draw-string bag of fate. The blank rune means death, according to the little booklet that comes with the set, but I hope he read a little further and learned that it could also mean the absolute end of something. The blank tile can actually be a positive sign: new beginning. Still, I don't expect it would have mattered what tile he drew, or what he thought it meant.

I don't expect it occurred to Victor to think of that old magazine cover, with a younger and hopeful-looking him patting a dog and listening with an expression of neutral pleasure to an unspecified music. But I find myself thinking, as I didn't when Victor's death was fresh, of the two images, the one of posed contentment, and the other of real-life squalor and misery—a middle-aged man letting a pretentious pop single contain and enlarge all his sense of failure.

Suicide rates go down in wartime. Isn't that a fascinating fact? Except that I can never work out what it means. Does it mean that people with a self-destructive streak volunteer for dangerous jobs or missions, so they don't need to go to the trouble of topping themselves—they're either killed or cured? Or does it mean that people forget to be self-obsessed when there's a genuine crisis out there in the world?

You'd think there'd be a lot of Aids-related suicides, but there aren't. It can't just be a matter of being British, not wanting to make a fuss, all that. There must be a few people who freak out when they're diagnosed HIV-positive out of a clear blue sky; they're the most likely to lay hands on themselves. But anyone who's already shown symptoms must at least have considered the possibility. Knowing the worst can even calm people down, in a certain sense.

It's different for people who are really sick. They're faced with a series of days only fractionally better or worse than the one before, and suicide is such an all-or-nothing business. It's really tricky deciding what individual trial finally tips a life over into being not worth the living, and then sticking to your decision. It's like a problem in algebra. What is x, such that x plus 1 is unbearable?

But how do the survivors feel if someone does commit suicide in the middle of a war? That was the problem for the Bears—that was what we were dropped in. We knew damn well that Victor wasn't physically sick. He couldn't have taken an HIV test without our knowing. It seemed to us that he'd just thrown away a body that any of our sick friends, any dwindling Bear, would have jumped at. OK, so Victor was short of puff, no great shakes when it came to running up stairs. There are plenty of skinny people who could have learned to put up with that.

We were angry. Didn't Victor know there was a war on? We Bears had given bouquets that had appeared at the graveside stripped of their messages. We had laboured to clean the bathrooms of the dead, so that their heirs found nothing so much as a stain to alarm them—and had had our names forgotten however many times we were introduced to them. We had held our candles high at Trafalgar Square vigils, year after year, forming helpful compositional groups on cue, for press photographs that never got published. And there was Victor beautiful in his coffin, plump in his coffin, his poison-blued face hardly presenting a challenge to the undertaker's cosmetician.

Everywhere we look we see Aids. We can be driving along, not thinking of anything. We stop at the traffic lights and there's a cyclist waiting there too, foot flexed on the pedal, ready to shoot off first. The picture of health. Except that he's wearing a mask to filter the city air that makes us think of an oxygen mask, and there's a personal stereo fastened by a strap to his bicep that reminds us of a drip feed—as if he was taking music intravenously.

So how could Victor see anything but Aids? What gave him the right to follow his obsession with his father so far? Somehow while we were all busy he found the time to invent his own illness. Wasn't Aids good enough for him? We loved his flesh, but it was unnatural that he died with it unmelted. Dying fat is an obscenity, these days. You're not supposed to be able to take it with you.

These days I understand Victor a little better. His anti-suicide note has made me understand suicide in a way that no suicide note could ever do. His father dying made his failure final. When we finally worked out the access code for his home computer, we found it was full of rambling journal entries saying so. But in another way he must have been relieved. With both his parents dead, he didn't need to resist the temptation of suicide any more, for their sake. He had no loyalty to life. He felt no patriotism for the mortal country.

I realize now that Victor's life only amounted to a little loop of track, like a child's first model railway layout. There was only one set of points in the whole circuit, and every time Victor passed it he had to decide whether to commit himself to going round again. But even if he did, he knew that he'd be passing the points again soon. Sooner or later he was bound to make the other choice.

He didn't steer the way we do. He wasn't affected by our weather. His despair was a gyroscope. But any other time, we would have grieved for him.

I didn't go to the memorial service, though I know that one or two of the Bears did, along with a couple of colleagues from work. But all the Bears turned up to a funeral feast at the Bromley house. We had a sort of picnic, but there was an ugly feeling behind it all, a resentment we didn't quite come out with. Most of us got a little drunk, which didn't help. I remember wandering through the house, looking for signs of Victor, even though I had helped so recently to clear such things away. I found a photo of him in a drawer, and slipped it into a pocket. Then a little later, someone dragged out the bin-bags of Victor's papers and possessions, and a little after that we made a bonfire.

Where else in 1991 could you see

Patricia Highsmith
Robertson Davies
Iris Murdoch
Peter Greenaway
Winnie Mandela
Hanif Kureishi
Oliver Sacks
Caryl Phillips
A S Byatt
Susan Sontag
Terry MacMillan
Howard Barker
and Andre Brink

ICΛTALKS

The Mall, London SW1
071 930 3647

NOTES FROM ABROAD

Brazil
Sue Halpern

Water curls through the Fortaleza slum: sewer water. It drains between shacks made of sticks and mud, and is pretty when it catches the sun. It gathers in 'Lagoa Porangabussu', which is not a lake but a cesspool where the locals swim. My companion, an American medical student, and I side-step boys shooting marbles, a sulky rooster and Renato the transvestite, who is shaving his legs. We meet a naked girl soaking in a metal tub, a man on horseback selling cow livers from wooden saddle-bags, a toddler drinking thick black coffee, a skinny, nervous dog, and a fellow no more than two feet tall, who is mostly chest and smiling face. 'Polio,' my companion says. He has come from the plague, leprosy and typhus wards at the Infectious Disease Hospital, where there is a man with the largest foot he has ever seen.

Cholera is expected soon in Brazil. In the spring of 1991 I was in upstate New York. As the disease spread from Peru to Ecuador, from Colombia to the Amazon, I tracked it on a map as if it were weather. I studied its history. In the Egyptian cholera epidemic of 1831, thirteen per cent of the population of Cairo died. Twenty-four years later, in Rio de Janeiro, 102,000 died in a single year. The cholera epidemic that devastated Cairo had originated five years earlier in Bengal, spread to southern Russia, followed Russian troops into Persia, Turkey and the Baltics, travelled by ship to England and Ireland, crossed to Canada and torn through North America. This year's outbreak in South America, where the disease had not been seen for a century, began somewhere else thirty years ago.

I called tropical disease specialists in Rio, public health experts in Atlanta and officials of the World Health Organization. A professor of medicine at the University of Virginia thought he knew where in Brazil cholera would strike first: Fortaleza, a north-eastern coastal city of two million. If the north-east were a separate country, he said, it would be the poorest state in South America after Bolivia. The people already suffered from diarrhoeal diseases at rates similar to those in Bangladesh. I set off for Fortaleza, a city I had not heard of before cholera.

I arrived in Monguba, a suburb. A nurse from the maternity hospital in Fortaleza was examining women and children. The patients sat quietly on wooden benches and fanned themselves with cholera pamphlets, which they did not know how to read.

No one in Monguba suffered from cholera yet. The first patient, Francisca, was thirty-three and pregnant with her seventh child. She was with José, her six-year-old son. She climbed on to a table and hiked her yellow cotton shift up to her breasts. José and I stared at his mother's mahogany belly, which was carved with deep, white lines from her other babies. The nurse listened to the foetal heart. 'You shouldn't smoke,' she said, lowering the dress. She gave Francisca two bottles: iron pills for herself, antibiotics for José. José had bloody stools from intestinal parasites. The next child, a three-year-old girl in a frilly pink party dress, also had parasites. Not cholera—just parasites under the surface of her skin, which was cross-hatched with thin red lines where the bugs were burrowing. The nurse gave her mother a bottle of iron pills and told her to dissolve them and rub the solution into the skin. The next child had scabies—not cholera—and was sweating pus. The next patient, a teenager, was pregnant, and had two kinds of worms, but not cholera. The little boy who followed her did not have cholera—still, he had lost half his body weight in six months. 'The water,' the nurse said later, explaining the diarrhoeas, the amoebas, the scabies and the worms, 'is very bad.' I went with her to another clinic, seven miles up the road. We stopped for popsicles, and sucked out their iciness, even though the cholera brochure we carried said we shouldn't. It was too hot not to.

The nurse distributed packets of oral rehydration salts, supplied by the Brazilian ministry of health, to patients with chronic diarrhoea. The packets are not in short supply, but will be when cholera comes. A person with cholera can wake up healthy and die at sundown. Diarrhoea and vomiting drain half the body's fluids. The victim shrivels and turns yellow and green. Capillaries break and the skin bruises, until the body can shrink no more and there is insufficient blood pressure for the heart to beat. But cholera is not fatal if it is treated early enough, and the treatment is simple and cheap. This year only one per cent of Peruvians who swallowed the cholera bacillus died from it, because the government distributed sufficient quantities of rehydration salts to hospitals and clinics. The salts, a mixture of sugar, salt and minerals, allow the body to maintain its electrolyte balance and to stave off dehydration in spite of losing fluid through diarrhoea and vomiting.

Dona Maria is ancient, bony and spry. She works as an attendant at the health post in Pavuna, another village outside of Fortaleza. It is a job for money, a dollar a day. Her true vocation, for which she refuses payment, is spiritualist healing. Although Dona Maria considers herself a devout Catholic, for thirty-five years she has been pinching parts of the Catholic liturgy, laying on hands, infusing herbs which she grows in her backyard. From visiting medical professors, she learned how to mix ordinary table salt and cane sugar into a drink that stops diarrhoea; now she prescribes this potion too.

'I cure you,' says Dona Maria to a diarrhoea sufferer. 'I cure you with the powers of God and the Virgin Mary.' She says this three times and chants one Our Father and one Hail Mary. Then she prepares and serves the sugar and salt tea. For cholera she says she will repeat the prayer nine times.

'*H*obby, Hobby,' a little boy calls out as we pick our way through the Fortaleza slum. My companion's name is Robert Newman—Robby. People here call him 'doctor', though he isn't a doctor but a third-year medical student. In the course of researching cryptosporidium, a chronic diarrhoeal disease, he has learned how to treat pneumonia, worms, measles and impetigo.

We walk to the house of eight-month-old Erivando, one of Robby's patients. Robby has treated his mother and the ten relatives and friends they live with. The house: two rooms, inadequate furnishings, a magazine portrait of Jesus on the wall, no place to pee, no running water, twelve occupants not counting the pig. My inventory stops when I see Erivando. He does not move or smile, does not blink or cry. His skin is grey. He is hollow and parched, like an old man. Erivando has dehydrating diarrhoea, and it has taken away his muscles and wasted his mind. Cholera has not yet arrived.

"WITHOUT" *Books*

A Cinema Without Walls
Movies and Culture After Vietnam
Timothy Corrigan, Temple University
How has the way we watch films changed as a result of modern advertising techniques, VCR's, cable TV, and coverage of the Vietnam war? Corrigan takes a close look at films such as *Blue Velvet, My Beautiful Laundrette* and *Paris, Texas*.
October 1991: 256pp: 234x156: illus. b+w photographs
Hb: 0-415-07133-X: £35.00
Pb: 0-415-07134-8: £9.99

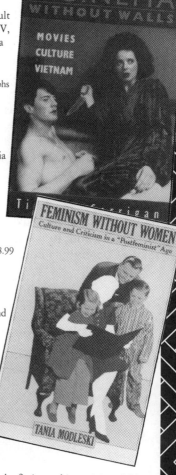

Feminism Without Women
Culture and Criticism in a 'Postfeminist' Age
Tania Modleski, University of Southern California
Examines 'postfeminism' in popular culture, especially popular film, and in cultural studies. Films covered range from *Three Men and a Baby* to *Lethal Weapon* and social issues from surrogate motherhood to lesbian S&M.
September 1991: 160pp: 234x156
Hb: 0-415-90416-1: £30.00 Pb: 0-415-90417-X: £8.99

Imperial Eyes
Travel Writing and Transculturation
Mary Louise Pratt, Stanford University
Explores European travel writing and economic and political expansion since 1700, showing how the domestic subject of European imperialism was created for the readership.
November 1991: 304pp: 234x156:
illus. 37 b+w photographs
Hb: 0-415-02675-X: £35.00
Pb: 0-415-06095-8: £10.99

Potboilers
Methods, Concepts and Case Studies in Popular Fiction
Jerry Palmer, City of London Polytechnic
Looks at the debate in the last two decades on popular fiction and its position within popular culture. The arguments are discussed with reference to crime fiction, soap opera, romance and TV sitcoms.
Communication and Society
November 1991: 240pp: 216x138
Hb: 0-415-00977-4: £35.00 Pb: 0-415-00978-2: £10.99

Available through all booksellers. In case of difficulty or for more information contact:
James Powell, Routledge, 11 New Fetter Lane, London EC4P 4EE.

ROUTLEDGE

GRANTA
LETTERS

Fuck

To the Editor

I feel compelled to write to you regarding the cover of issue 37, which arrived last evening. I eagerly tore open the plastic wrapper, sorted through the various inserts you had thoughtfully placed over the title page, read about the change of address for subscriber services and then there it was.

I have never laughed as hard at the cover of a periodical in my adult life, neither the *National Review* nor the *National Enquirer* have elicited such mirth. I promptly showed it to my wife, who stole the issue and started reading it.

Because of her petty larceny I can't comment on the issue's content, though I am sure it meets or exceeds your usual excellent standards. I am sure too, based on your cover art, that I will enjoy and be able to empathize with almost every page.

I hope that you don't receive too many unpleasant reactions to the cover. I loved it, and I now have one more reason to subscribe to *Granta*.

Sean Skilling
New York

To the Editor

I can see some of the possible arguments in favour of your miserable cover slogan: perhaps it is avant-garde, or legitimate because it quotes Philip Larkin; and, after all, it has served its purpose by shocking me. Yet I am shocked, not because you descend to the feeblest level of street language, but because you and your staff were not more articulate or subtle about it.

No doubt you don't see yourselves as custodians of anything in particular, let alone old-fashioned standards of writing. No doubt literary modernism means being realistic, and that is how people talk nowadays. But the root of the problem is extremism: as if you can't have a good literary magazine unless the cover swears at you, or a good travel story unless it beats Redmond O'Hanlon being drugged by a tribe of man-eating Indians and having his penis stuck by spiny fish, or a good piece of modern realism unless it is steeped in boredom, violence and disillusionment. In pursuit of the great god Profit have you perhaps lost sight of the inner values of literature, which are not a function of cheap sensation (or the feeblest utterances of the big names)? I think you may have fucked it up this time.

Dr David Alexander
Amherst, MA

To the Editor

This is too much. I'm as aware as you are of the sadness, misery and bestiality of the human condition, but you go on and on and on as if there were nothing else. Have you ever tried psychoanalysis? Or faith in something other than your own biliousness?

Stanley A Leary M.D.
New Haven
Connecticut

To the Editor

I have been reading *Granta* for some five years. It was with shock that I received your latest volume, opened, by my eight- and ten-year-old sons. 'What does this mean?' was the question. They know that 'fuck' is not a word to be used, so they not unnaturally wondered what it was doing on the front cover of a book.

I feel strongly enough about this not to want this book in my proud collection and I am returning it forthwith. Perhaps you can return it with a different cover, so that I can enjoy the writing inside?

Richard Ellison
Loughborough

To the Editor

I have long been a fan of your magazine and I have used several of your issues with my A-level English students, with great success (I am thinking particularly of the superb writing in the issues on Travel Writing, or of James Fenton's reportage in Saigon). However, the cover design for *Granta* 37 reads like something out of the *News of the World* and guarantees that, no matter how enlightened and educational the actual writing is within the covers,

this issue cannot be used in schools. Well-read adults like you and I can appreciate the reference to Larkin's poem which makes an ironic use of demotic English, but this is lost on the average seventeen-year-old (or on his/her parents). When I compare the tawdry cover of *Granta* 37 to the superb covers of earlier *Granta*s, I can only conclude that you no longer employ the same people in your art department.

R A May
Head of English
Boswells School
Chelmsford

To the Editor

Whilst I agree with the sentiments behind the comment on the cover of the latest *Granta* that families 'fuck you up', I find it unfortunate that you have made the statement so obvious.

As one who is trying hard to bring up young children so that they do not become fucked up, I will find it difficult to leave this copy of your otherwise excellent publication lying around; as this is one of the words whose use I seek to discourage, how can I justify my attitude when it appears so openly on the cover of your publication? At least, in the *Guardian*, etc, fuck is usually buried in a long paragraph, not printed as a headline.

John Tiratsoo
Beaconsfield

Disinformation

To the Editor

I doubt very much that this letter will do any good, but I was so saddened by *Granta* 36 that I feel compelled to write. 'Election Night in Nicaragua' by Sergio Ramirez grossly misrepresents the facts in some crucial aspects; indeed it could reasonably be classified as disinformation. His article is tragically flawed, as the following demonstrably false statements illustrate:

'The revolution pardoned Somoza's thugs—there were no firing-squads, gallows or guillotines and many fled to Honduras or Miami. . .'

This is half right. Somoza's thugs escaped vengeance only because they had money to buy airline tickets out of the country. The majority of Nicaraguans, mostly poor peasants, were stuck there. And they bore the brunt of Sandinist vengeance. Throughout the decade the Sandinists ruled, it was difficult to ascertain the extent of mass killings perpetrated by the Sandinist Army. Now the truth is slowly trickling out. Consider the following interview, published this summer, with Raoul Shade, who has documented Sandinist Army abuses ever since he was thrown out of El Salvador for documenting the human rights abuses of the Salvadoran Army: [says Shade:]

'I'm interested in human rights. If you're interested in human rights, you clash with all sides,'
'How long—'
—'did it take me to start hating the Sandinists?' he finished the question for me. 'About six months. That's about how long it took for the peasants to start trusting me. And when they trusted me, they started telling me about the cemeteries.'

Each one holds from ten to sixty bodies, the corpses of peasants who were summarily executed as suspected contra collaborators. Shade was stunned at first— human-rights organizations and the international press corps, which were going at the abuses of the Salvadoran government with hammer and tongs, had been silent on the subject of Nicaragua—but he heard the stories from so many peasants that he had to believe them. Yet there was nothing he could do; most of the cemeteries were located near Sandinist military bases where it would be impossible to turn the earth without attracting unwelcome attention. So he took careful notes and waited. In June 1990, less than two months after Violeta Chamorro took office, he dug up his first burial ground. Since then he's uncovered nine more.

'What I don't understand,' says Shade, 'is why there isn't more interest in the story. If someone finds graves of people killed by the military governments in Argentina or Chile, then the whole world demands an investigation. But here, I can't even get anybody to donate a used jeep and a few tanks of gas.'

And for the exiles—contras, middle-class professionals, Somoza thugs—who have come home, there is the danger of the vengeance of the Sandinists. While the international media widely reported the murder of ex-contra leader Enrique Bermudez—shot in the back in February in the parking lot of the Inter-Continental Hotel—what has gone unnoticed is that prominent opponents of the Sandinists are being murdered at the rate of one every five days. Check with Americas Watch. So far this year that human rights organization has documented over fifty murders of former contras. It is obvious that if Somoza's thugs were safe, it is because they were not within reach.

'No more wheat for Nicaragua: there was suddenly an embargo on trade. No more loans for Nicaragua: there was suddenly a financial blockade.'

True and unfortunate and shameful. But Mr Ramirez doesn't tell the entire story. Aid came pouring in—and not just from the Soviet Union, Cuba and the PRC. Mexico under Lopez Portillo gave the Sandinist government 1.5 *billion* dollars in aid over a three year period. Venezuela and Mexico also jointly provided oil, free of charge. The Spanish, Italians, French, Germans and Scandinavians also helped out. An enormous activist network in the US and Canada emerged, giving

school supplies, trucks, tractors, money, volunteers. Californians, especially, made summers of picking cotton and coffee in Nicaragua, building schools and teaching peasants, laying down pipelines and smuggling Nicaraguan goods into America. Nicaragua was never alone.

'A few days later we discovered some empty offices in the Central Bank . . . It was as if everything had been miraculously awaiting us: desks, filing-cabinets, telephones, typewriters, a porcelain coffee service inscribed with the Central Bank insignia . . .'

Mr Ramirez was more fortunate than Mrs Chamorro. When she arrived, she discovered that everything—including the toilet in the presidential office—had been removed. In fact, the looting perpetuated by the outgoing Sandinists was so great that Nicaraguans refer to the two-month transition period between governments as the 'great *piñata*': the Sandinists broke open the national treasury and took off with all the goodies.

'. . . the first Somoza's men . . . would appear at the sales auctioning repossessed estates—cattle ranches, coffee plantation—and buy them up for next-to-nothing . . .'

Mr Ramirez knows his history well, presumably, so he and the Sandinist leadership could see how it was done.

Indeed, during the transition period government bank accounts were systematically emptied. In one instance an account at the Central Bank was emptied of twenty-four million dollars, which at the time represented over forty per cent of all the money in circulation in the country. Check with the Nicaraguan Central Bank—they're still trying to find out who took it. No one doubts it was the Sandinists, but they want to see if they can get some of it back. What frustrates the government now, however, is not that they don't know where the money is, but that there's not much to recover. Consider three Sandinist business ventures: a Sandinist-backed airline that is quickly losing so much money it has had to discontinue passenger service, and even now its cargo operations hardly pay the bills; the Sandinist Pacific beach resort—built at the Somoza beach estate the revolutionary government confiscated in the 'national' interest, which was quickly 'privatized' right before it left office—which is empty; and a television station that never went on the air because the Sandinist owners have been unable to sell any advertising.

'I was thinking of this recently when the new mayor of Managua celebrated taking office in the gardens of the Intercontinental Hotel. He had also been a judge under Somoza and had sentenced many Sandinists to his jails . . . Among those present . . . Adolfo Calero, leader of the counter-revolutionaries.'

What Mr Ramirez fails to mention is that the Mayor of Managua, Arnoldo Aleman, won his office in a free election. What Mr Ramirez, too, fails to mention is that the Sandinists absolutely despise Mr Aleman precisely because Mr Aleman has called the Sandinists frauds for years and as Mayor he has shown off his contempt for them. For example, the enormous Hollywood-style 'FSLN' letters on the mountains overlooking the capital were changed to read, 'FIN', Spanish for 'The End'. Then they were unceremoniously taken down altogether. Mr Aleman has also earned Mr Ramirez's wrath by having the city paint over Sandinist murals all over town, and—the final insult—claiming that since the city's coffers were looted by the outgoing Sandinist mayor and budget cuts are in order, the eternal flame that burns over the tomb of Carlos Fonesca, the founder of the Sandinist party, was turned off. So far few complaints have been received by the Mayor's office from the people who live in the city of Managua.

And as for Adolfo Calero, Mr Ramirez fails to mention that this man, unlike the ousted Sandinists, is hardly making trouble. 'I've had my picture in the *New York Times* magazine and all over the world, and so what?' Adolfo Calero, one of the top contra politicians, told an American interview recently, 'I'm still a beginner here. I'm a lot poorer, a lot less established, a lot less everything than I was in 1982 when I left the country.' And what precisely is Mr Calero up to these days? He's the Nicaraguan representative of an Italian construction company, making money by earning it. His goal is to start a fruit-juice bottling company (before the revolution he was a Coca-Cola bottler). Mr Calero plans to sell orange, apple and mango juice by next year. If only all Nicaraguans were engaged in productive activities . . .

'After losing last year's election, we realized that no Sandinist militants, whether ministers of state or grassroots activists, had any possessions . . . We then passed a law granting the title deeds of all state-owned properties to the families living in them . . . the houses were either given free or sold on mortgages . . .'

A rather nice gesture. But this begs the question: What if the state took possession of a property illegally? Consider just one case of one Sandinist: Daniel Ortega. Glenn Garvin, an American who has been in Nicaragua for some time, and whose new book examines the impact of the 'great *piñata*' on the Chamorro government, reports the following:

'The best-known house in Managua is one that hardly anybody has seen in years. It's the mansion where Daniel Ortega lives. The house belongs to Amparo Morales, a Mexican woman who fled Nicaragua during the final days of the revolution to escape the violence. She returned a few weeks later, and when she opened the front door, there stood Rosario

Murillo, Ortega's wife, wearing one of Amparo's bathrobes. That was the last time Amparo set foot in her own house—the revolutionary government had confiscated it, she learned, on the grounds that her husband was a wealthy Nicaraguan banker. (No matter that he had a long and distinguished history of opposition to the Somoza dynasty that the Sandinists had just toppled.) Soon after, a twenty-foot-high wall went up around the house, completely hiding it from view.

When the Sandinists lost the election in 1990, Amparo Morales returned to Nicaragua in the hope that the new government would return her house. But it seems the government no longer owns the million-dollar mansion: Daniel Ortega bought it during the *piñata* at a five-fingered discount price of 1,000 dollars. Since then, Amparo's efforts to shame him into leaving the digs have been daily headlines in the Managua papers. She even got the Mexican ambassador to write Ortega a reproving letter, although the fact that the Mexican Embassy itself is located in a confiscated mansion didn't exactly cloak the ambassador in moral authority.

One morning I asked my taxi driver to take me to the Ortega house. "The Morales house," he reprimanded me, as we set off. "And it's not a house, either." When we arrived, I saw what he meant. It's a two-square-block compound. In the guard posts atop the walls, I counted more than two dozen soldiers armed with automatic rifles.

"Why would the army be guarding Daniel Ortega?" I asked the driver. "He has no connection to the government now."

"That's the way it is here," the driver sniffed. "The Sandinists think they still run everything." As we drove away, he added: "And they're right. They do run everything, because they have all the guns."

He was referring to Daniel's brother Humberto, who still commands the Nicaraguan army. The Chamorro government's decision to retain him has been a hugely unpopular one, all the more so since his bodyguards gunned down a Managua teenager who had the effrontery to try to pass the general's motorcade with his vehicle.'

A California firm, ICM, estimates there are over 150,000 similar cases. It is the same kind of nightmare that faces Eastern Europe and the Soviets—and will face Cuba at some point.

'Before midnight an emergency session of the Sandinist leadership agreed that the election results must be respected.'

How generous. As if they had a choice. What were they going to do? Steal the election and have Jimmy Carter, Joao Baena Soares of the OAS, Elliot Richardson of the UN and representatives of Amnesty International, Americas Watch and dozens of news agencies report an electoral fraud to the entire world? It would have been the perfect excuse for the Americans to launch a Grenada or Panama operation. Mr Ramirez had no choice in the matter, so there is no point in taking the credit for doing what is inevitable.

'He reminded everyone that we had no intention of clinging to power, and that we were leaving office as poor as when we had arrived.'

Mr Ortega, to my knowledge, did not own a one million dollar home when he came to power. And during the tense months leading up to the Persian Gulf War, he criss-crossed Europe, northern Africa and the Middle East trying to work out the differences between Saddam Hussein and George Bush. Who picked up the tab—87,000 dollars—if none other than his very own banker, who is under pressure now because he has been linked to the BCCI affair. If the Sandinists left office as poor as when they arrived, it seems difficult to believe their members could squander tens of thousands of dollars on first-class airline tickets and fancy hotel rooms.

I could go on, but I would be redundant. My point is this: *Granta* should not let itself be used for propaganda shenanigans such as these. The tragic truth about the Sandinist Revolution in Nicaragua is that it is not complete. Nicaragua is a small country, and her people must heal their wounds. The Somoza years are horrible— the product of America's relentless imperialist tendencies—but the Sandinists who replaced the dictator proved themselves to be as despotic as Somoza himself. Daniel

Ortega spends his days in a house stolen from a private, foreign citizen whose husband opposed Somoza. The Sandinist leadership—who imposed strict censorship when they were in power—now denounce proposed pornography laws that would undermine their only lucrative post-Sandinist venture: *operating a chain of porn theatres in Managua.* Meanwhile, the Chamorro government struggles to revive a brain-dead economy, while the Sandinist Army is hunting down its former enemies. Americas Watch is growing alarmed at the growing violence, and the situation is deteriorating so rapidly that former contras are becoming active once more. It is, indeed, an enormous mess.

I should like to point out that I am not a contra, or a Sandinist. I'm not even Nicaraguan. I am a Mexican citizen from Mérida, Yucatán, who is presently in Washington on business related to the negotiations for a free-trade agreement between the US, Canada and Mexico. But although I am not Nicaraguan, I am very concerned about this article because it diminishes the respect for *Granta* that I have always had. I am sure many readers share my concern. I would like to see an explanation or clarification. It is unfortunate and it saddens me that *Granta*'s publishing Sergio Ramirez's article will do little to heal the wounds of Nicaragua and—worst—it further distorts the facts to the international community.

Louis E.V. Nevaer
Washington, D.C.

To the Editor

Sergio Ramirez's article seemed to me not to pretend to be anything other than what it was: a piece written with considerable literary licence by an important partisan in the Nicaraguan conflict. I did not think of it as a piece that purported to tell what actually happened; only as a piece that gave his view of what happened. Accordingly, it did not seem to me important to assess it accordingly to the standards that would be required of an historian or of a human rights organization. As to the specific criticisms by Mr Nevaer, I can only respond to those that touch on human rights matters. I comment in the order that they are touched on in Mr Nevaer's letter:

1. Vengeance against 'Somoza's thugs'; clandestine cemeteries.
These are actually two separate matters. The Sandinistas did not execute those associated with the previous regime. They did imprison several thousands of them, after trials before special tribunals that lacked many elements of procedural fairness. There were some isolated vengeance killings at the moment of the triumph of the revolution, but no one has established that there was a policy or practice of such killings. On the other hand, there is no indication that those responsible for the killings that did take place were prosecuted and punished.

As for clandestine cemeteries, a dozen of these have been identified since the Chamorro government came into office. The forensic work has not been done in enough cases to be certain exactly how many bodies these contain or who was responsible for killing those buried in them. ANPDH, a group funded by the US State Department as part of its support for the contras that was supposed to promote improvements in the human rights practices of the contras, attributes ten of the cemeteries to the Sandinistas, two to the contras. In all, there appear to be some ninety bodies in the cemeteries attributed to the Sandinistas. As far as we have been able to establish, those buried there were suspected contras or contra collaborators or draft resisters executed by the Sandinistas. That is, they are of more recent vintage than Mr Nevaer suggests and the numbers are not so high as those he attributes to Raoul Shade. These executions were gross abuses of human rights and the Sandinistas deserve denunciation for these and other abuses not mentioned by Mr Nevaer.

2. Vengeance against returning exiles—'contras, middle class professionals, Somoza thugs.'
By last July, we were aware of some fifty-two killings of persons in these categories, but most of these do not warrant the use of the word 'murders'. Most involve armed confrontations between Sandinistas and former contras, with disputes over property touching off much of this violence. Culpability is often difficult to determine. One case which certainly was a murder was the killing of Enrique Bermudez, but it is far from clear who was responsible. It might have been Sandinistas, but it might have been his enemies within the contra movement.

Comandos, a new book by Sam Dillon, a reporter for *The Miami Herald*, is an excellent account of violence within the *contra* movement. It provides a lot of information about the enemies of Mr Bermudez.

3. Adolfo Calero
Mr Nevaer's description of Calero portrays him as a peaceful businessman—formerly a Coca-Cola bottler, now a marketer of fruit juices. At best, this is a partial picture.

My first visit to Managua was in August 1981. I happened to arrive on the same flight as a prominent academic expert on Latin America whom I knew to be closely associated with the CIA. He had been involved in the overthrow of the Allende regime in Chile. On the plane, he told me that a Nicaraguan friend was to meet him at the airport and offered me a ride with that person to the hotel at which we were both staying. The Nicaraguan friend to whom he introduced me was Calero, then a Coca-Cola bottler. Shortly thereafter, Calero left Nicaragua to head what became the contras.

Sam Dillon's book, mentioned above, has a lot to say about Calero's role in attempting to cover up the grossest human rights abuses by the contras. Dillon's account is completely consistent with the experience of Americas Watch.

4. Sandinista decision to respect the elections.
Actually, I thought that Ramirez's account was very frank as he acknowledged that this was in doubt. I agree with Mr Nevaer that the Sandinistas had little choice, but at other times they had done things which seemed highly improbable.

A minor point: the references to Americas Watch and Amnesty International in this context are misleading. Amnesty does not monitor elections; and though Americas Watch had observers present, they were not there to monitor the fairness of the elections, only the possibility of election-related violence. The election monitors were the others mentioned by Mr Nevaer.

Aryeh Neier
Executive Director
Human Rights Watch
New York

Notes on Contributors

Bill Morris grew up in Detroit, Michigan, and has worked as a newspaper reporter in Washington, D.C., and a disc jockey in Nashville, Tennessee. He now lives in North Carolina and writes a weekly column for the *Greensboro News and Record*. He owns two 1954 Buicks. 'Motorama 1954' is his first published fiction. It will be included in *Biography of a Buick*, a novel, that will be published in Britain by Granta Books, and in the United States by Alfred A. Knopf, in the spring. **Jeremy Rifkin** is best known for his environmental work and his critique of modern technologies. His books include *Biosphere Politics*, *Time Wars* and *Algeny*. He is the president of the Greenhouse Crisis Foundation and of the Foundation on Economic Trends. 'Anatomy of a Cheeseburger' is adapted from *Beyond Beef, The Rise and Fall of the Cattle Culture*, which will be published in the spring in the United States by E.P.Dutton. **Ivan Klíma**'s story may have been inspired by the Railwaymen's Ball held in Prague on 28 January 1978 that resulted in the arrest of Vaclav Havel and other members of Charter '77. Havel was charged with interfering with a police officer in the course of his duties and was held until 13 March. *My Golden Trades*, a collection of interrelated stories based on events in Czechoslovakia of the last ten years, will be published by Granta Books in April 1991. **Tracy Kidder** is the author of three important books of non-fiction: *Among Schoolchildren*, *House* and *The Soul of a New Machine*, for which he won the Pulitzer Prize. 'The Adjuster' is his first published fiction. **Eugene Richards**'s previous photo stories in *Granta* include 'Amazon', an account of his wife's unsuccessful struggles with cancer (*Granta* 16), and 'Emergency Room', an account of the emergency operating room at Denver General Hospital (*Granta* 27). **Louise Erdrich** was born in 1954. She is the author of four novels and one book of poems. She lives in New Hampshire with her husband, fellow writer Michael Dorris. **Adam Mars-Jones**, who was also born in 1954, has published two collections of short stories. *Monopolies of Loss*, a new collection which includes stories first published in *Granta*, will appear in the spring. **Sue Halpern** lives in New York. Her first book, *Migrations to Solitude,* will be published in February.

In 1989 the death penalty was re-introduced in Britain. Not for murder. Not for terrorism. But for writing a book.

On the 14th February 1989 sentence of death was pronounced on a British citizen, living in this country.

It was not handed down by a British Court of Law. Nor did it have the authority of the British parliament.

It was decreed by a foreign government – the government of Iran.

The "crime" which they deemed worthy of the ultimate penalty was the writing of a book.

On November 11th 1991, the author of the book, Salman Rushdie, will have lived under this threat to his life for one thousand days.

There is no dispute that the book is controversial. Many people have admired it, and it has won literary prizes in Britain, Italy and Germany.

On the other hand certain passages have offended some (but not all) Muslims.

In this country, however, people are not killed for writing controversial books.

There is no death penalty in British Law.

To millions of people this threat to the life of an innocent man is deeply offensive.

It is important that such people make their feelings known. Not by issuing violent threats, but by the free, legal and democratic expression of their views.

Each one of us is free to write to a member of government or the British Foreign Secretary Douglas Hurd.

We can ensure that Salman Rushdie's plight is not allowed to be forgotten.

We can demand that the desire of governments to secure lucrative overseas contracts is not allowed to take precedence over the removal of an unlawful threat to the life of a British citizen.

And we can remind Douglas Hurd that if threats of this kind are seen to prevail, it will not be long before the very democracy that elected him to office is also threatened.

JOIN THE SHOW OF SUPPORT TO MARK THE 1000TH DAY OF SALMAN RUSHDIE'S ORDEAL.